D1519961

DOCUMENTS
TO MANAGE BY

DOCUMENTS
TO MANAGE BY

Leslie H. Matthies

Management Research Society

OFFICE PUBLICATIONS, INC.
1200 Summer Street, Stamford, CT 06904

ISBN Number: 0–911054-06-5

Library of Congress Catalog Card Number :82-81937

Matthies, Leslie H.
  Documents to Manage By

Indexing
  1. Documents 2. Management 3. Organizational Charts
  4. Authority Patterns 5. Policy 6. Procedure

CONTENTS

NUGGETS ON MANAGEMENT
FROM THE WORLD'S GREATEST BOOK

And thou shalt teach them (the people) ordinances and laws, and shalt show them the way wherein they must walk, and the work that they must do.

Exodus 18:20

Not slothful in business; fervent in spirit, serving the Lord.

Romans 12:11

For GOD is not the author of confusion, but of peace . . .

I Corinthians 14:33

INTRODUCTION

Decisions cost money because members of management make up our most expensive group of employees. Further, their time for doing work is always in short supply.

A decision, once made, can be an asset. Or it can be frittered away and essentially the same decision may be made again tomorrow, next week, next month, or next year. Decisions fall into two classifications:

1. Those that can be reused profitably.
2. Those that are of the moment.

Supervisors, staff people, and rank-and-file workers are making the second type of decision all day long. The first category of decisions is different because they have *long-range value.* It is this type of decision and the documents that reflect them that we consider in this book.

EXAMPLE: The top executives decide that only officially designated buyers may contact suppliers and order goods from them. That decision has long-range impact. A small group of engineers in a high-priority research project find that the basic decision (and quite appropriate for the normal situation) will slow them down to the point that their schedule will slip. Buyers in the Materiel division cannot accept rush orders on everything. So they work routinely, using well-defined systems channels.

Now what? Perhaps an exception is required, allowing one or two engineers to procure whatever is needed. Or should a professional buyer be detached from Materiel and assigned to the project team? Decisions. Decisions.

People in an organization work hard at communicating with each other. They soon find that communication that cascades down the chain of command is relatively ineffective. Consequently people's lateral contacts (face to face) are rampant, mostly in the form of meetings.

Such meetings are unceasing. People hold a hundred of them a day. Do these represent today's quota of short-term decisions? Maybe a thousand of them? The day is all too short. What should be done today probably won't get done, even tomorrow. QUESTION: Could there be less of such hectic activity if people could refer to a relatively few long-range decisions?

That is the question that this book addresses. Those longer-range decisions are often carried on documents that could help in the management process. But sadly, for the most part, they are not much help.

The decisions that do have long-range usefulness include decisions on *policy* . . . on *organization* structure . . . on the assignment of *departmental responsibilities* . . . on the most important (big show) *procedures* . . . and finally on the *authority to approve* pattern.

To make such long-range decisions useful in the future they must be reduced to writing, documented, and distributed to the men and women who need such guidance.

The quality of such management documents is so universally poor that instead of being used fully they are largely ignored. Organization charts, for example, are looked down upon by many executives and by observers of management practices.

Statements of work, which are "job descriptions" of departments, do not exist in some companies. In others where they do exist, they're often ignored because they are not in a useful form. Most such documents that do exist are poorly conceived, poorly written, and unwisely distributed.

Can we do better? The answer is positively YES! While dozens of management documents do exist, in this book we will give our attention to:

Organization charts
Statements of work

Policy statements

"Big show" procedures
Authority to approve patterns

Titles

It is my conviction, based on considerable personal experience, that when these documents are developed as *useful decision guides,* they become powerful management tools. They can provide a base for the myriad of daily decisions. Those five documents can be truly DOCUMENTS TO MANAGE BY. They can:

1. Guide people.
2. Order people.
3. Instruct people.
4. Ask people.
5. Change previous information.
6. Add a responsibility.
7. Alter an authority.
8. Inform people.
9. Warn people.
10. Inquire of people.
11. Train people.
12. Issue a notice.
13. Explain a situation.
14. Inform on a staff change.

The common goal of management documents can be summed up as aids to TEAMWORK. That's what all the personal activity is about . . . seeking teamwork. That's the reason that people hold so many meetings, make all the studies and surveys, confer with each other, and make those thousands of inside telephone calls.

Ignorance is rarely an asset; significant knowledge always is. So we ask, "If there are no management documents that reveal the organization structure, or the assigned functions, or the long-range goal, or the basic top decisions, or the responsibilities for results, or the authorities to approve ... how can people in the organization *know* about such matters?"

Chapter 1

THE SAD STATE OF
MANAGEMENT DOCUMENTS

Managers, supervisors, and staff people spend an average of 50 percent of their time in meetings. Their aim: coordination of effort. Naturally the communication mediums in those meetings are the eye and the ear. People speak and they listen. The subjects discussed may be summarized as minutes . . . one form of documentation.

Documentation, like those personally attended meetings, also aims at the coordination of human effort. However, most current *written* management documentation represents a relatively weak form of communication. Could it be better? That's the question we consider in this book.

You've probably seen dozens of different documents that well-meaning people write and distribute. You may have seen:

Policies . . . circular letters . . . announcements . . . organization charts . . . notices . . . executive directives . . . rules . . . organization change announcements . . . a president's letter . . . safety bulletins . . . a quality control letter . . . procedures . . . work instructions . . . and memos covering a variety of subjects. Just to name a few written pieces.

1. FIVE MAJOR DOCUMENTS

For the more enduring forms of written communication, management people use these five major documents:

1. Organization charts   4. Procedures
2. Statements of work   5. Authority to
3. Policy statements   approve patterns

Policies, procedures, and organization charts are fairly well known. However, "statements of work" go under a variety of titles. In many organizations such statements do not even exist. Well, *what* is a statement of work? To move from the known to the not-so-well-known, we could describe a statement of work as the "job description of a department." Other titles for statements of work include "functional outlines" and "responsibility and authority directives."

Fundamental to all other management documentation is the statement of the company's *goals*, a document that is rarely formalized. After all, if you don't know where the organization wants to go, how can you organize to go there?

2. TOOLS FOR THINKING

The five major documents can serve both as guides and as thinking tools for managers and supervisors. Those documents provide information that answers such questions as:

- ☐ *Who* is in charge of *what* work?
- ☐ *Who* reports to *whom?*
- ☐ What *policies* apply to a specific subject?
- ☐ How does DEPARTMENT "A" *coordinate* its efforts with DEPARTMENT "B"?
- ☐ How many organized *sub-units* are there?
- ☐ What *work* does each sub-unit do?
- ☐ How do they *relate?*
- ☐ *Who* has the right to *approve* what?

People can learn the answers to such questions by "osmosis" . . . by slowly absorbing the information, by bumbling and stumbling around. Then when management does make a change, without documentation how long does the supervisor or worker take to find out about that change?

Each of the five major documents can be highly useful to people who need to know who does what work and where. The documents can be *powerful thinking* tools for a manager when it comes to considering the working structure . . . or when considering the work that *groups* of people do. And all executives need a clear picture of the major arenas of action . . . the company's "big show" systems.

While this book will concentrate on the five major documents, it will also consider the key terms and titles used on the documents, including those of people, of the organization's subelements, and titles of the management documents. Other pertinent subjects include document distribution and control . . . and the document developer.

A policy statement is better known than are statements of work. However, the trouble with policy is that many so-called policies are communicated poorly . . . so poorly that people violate policy without realizing they are doing so. Other documents entitled "policy" are not policy at all. One large corporation announces all staff changes (from five to 20 a month) on a "policy" bulletin.

3. ANY VALUE IN MANAGEMENT DOCUMENTS?

The value of currently used management documents can vary from useless to quite useful. On a scale from 0 (useless) to 10 (extremely helpful) I would rate most documents between 1 and 5. The writers, executives, or their staff assistants, do not think out the purpose of each document. Neither do they provide a correct pattern of distribution. They couldn't tell you who makes up the "audience" or the readership.

Many current documents are an inconsistent mixture. They include items of temporary interest such as an extra holiday for the plant, or early closing because of an unexpected storm, or a breakdown of the electric power when the organization cannot provide ventilation or cooling. These are mixed with documents that could be useful for years such as a policy on conflicts of interest, on sales contacts . . . or on accepting gifts, lunches, and other favors from vendors.

Frequently an executive who feels that he must communicate

with the operating people on a subject uses the common office
memo. But who keeps memos? What is the real purpose of an
inter-office memo? If that executive has no standardized bulletin for each communicative purpose, what else can he use? Once
a subject of permanent interest does go out as a memo, where do
people file it? If the information must be revised later, who gets
copies of the new memo?

The weaknesses of the current crop of written management
documents are so numerous that it may seem hopeless to try to
do better . . . to bring some sensible order into such a chaotic
area.

Much of the writing is ponderous, vague, and general. The
document can't just be read: it must be studied. But busy people
will not study. Consequently many intended readers do not read
such documents. The conscientious few who do read them cannot understand them.

Some information going out on a bulletin or on a memo conflicts with previously issued information. Contrary information,
from two different offices, can go out at the same time. This
"documental crazy quilt" situation exists because:

1. No one has ever thought out the specific purpose
    of each document.

2. The writer mixes temporary information with in-
    formation of permanent value.

3. The writer does not write clearly.

4. The bulletins are not distributed to the people
    who can use the information.

5. The reader does not know how to respond or
    cannot understand what the writer wants.

6. Too much information with permanent value
    goes out as memos.

7. A thought out "family" of management docu-
    ments does not exist.

8. The documents that do exist have been so poorly
    handled that no one pays any attention to them.

9. The information is updated only in fits and
    starts.

The foregoing is a summary of the average management document situation. THOSE DOCUMENTS CAN BE IMPROVED ! So let's consider one such document at a time. First, let's give our attention to the organization chart. What is it? Who issues it? Who reads it? What values could it provide?

Chapter 2

ORGANIZATION CHARTS

Like other management documents, organization charts are usually of such poor quality that some people think of them as being disreputable. But we'll use the term "poor quality." The charts stress the wrong things. There are no design standards, they are poorly distributed and most of them do not reflect a current picture of the organization's human structure. They are plainly out of date.

1. WHY ORGANIZATION CHARTS ARE DESPISED

The size of the organization is no guarantee of chart quality. Some charts used in the Fortune 500 companies are confusing nightmares of boxes and lines.

You can judge a chart's quality only by its usefulness to the person who reads it. Does it provide a clear picture of the organization's working structure? Most charts have one or more of the following weaknesses. Some charts include every "bad" feature:

1. The chart developer tried to show too much on a single sheet of paper. The result is an unclear picture of the organization's structure.

2. The chart shows many sizes of boxes. Obviously there are no standards.

3. The chart includes high-sounding department titles (euphemisms) that have no real meaning to the reader and do not reflect the real work responsibility. EXAMPLE: *Contract Administration,* which should be called *Marketing.*

4. Other charts confuse the readers by using "people titles" that are not logical. EXAMPLE: The title of "manager" applied to someone with no one to manage.

5. The developer has scattered both group titles and individual titles throughout the chart.

6. The "language" of the chart is not consistent. It is obvious that no one has developed any charting standards. In one box a person's name dominates. In another the executive's title stands out. One box is made up of thick lines, another of thin lines. One box is square, another rectangular, still another isn't a box. It's round.

7. The developer has used unexplained dotted lines. Dotted lines represent his or her attempt to show what *cannot be shown* on a chart . . . lateral relationships. Lateral relationships can be of two types . . . personal, the eyeball-to-eyeball contact . . . or formal relationships explained in the procedures that reflect the various systems. Charts cannot show either.

8. Exaggeration or stretching the truth. In one basic chart for a large company, the staff analyst (the one who did the charting) supervised two people. However, he made his box appear as though it were a major department, equivalent to the production department, which had over 1400 employees. Such distortion destroyed the credibility of the entire chart.

9. Deliberate misrepresentation. The developer shows a box or a title to represent a work function that does not exist.

10. Lack of standards on widths and sizes of the rectangular boxes that depict the functions.

11. Emphasis on the work responsibilities that do not reflect the key or the "big show" function.*

12. Using an unexplained variety of thick, thin, or dotted lines to depict the relationships between the people shown in the boxes.

13. Failing to distinguish between a box that depicts staff work as opposed to line work responsibilities.

14. Inconsistent titles for managers and for work groups . . . sometimes using popular terms instead of official titles.

15. Overcrowding a chart. Failing to use the "peel-off technique" to show the complex organization structure of a large organization or of a large department.

16. Emphasizing something other than work, such as people's names or their titles. EXAMPLES: John Henry or Maria Bonatto . . . vice-president or director.

17. Putting too much detail on charts, such as listing all employees names right down to the rank-and-file employee.

Those facets of poor quality in charting can be eliminated if the person developing the charting recognizes that he or she is seeking to develop a useful management tool . . . a *document to manage by!* Such usefulness can be achieved if the developer adheres to a few simple charting principles, then develops a standard language for all charting.

2. SHOWING TOO MUCH ON A CHART

We've seen many bad charts, but the extreme (that we have encountered) must be these "before and after" charts issued by the

*The "big show" refers to the major work of the organization.

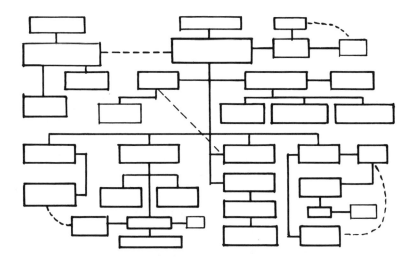

An overly complex chart is a poor quality chart. It is
not useful because the "picture" of the structure is not
clear. If any organization's structure really looked like
the above, heaven help it!

United States Department of Health, Education and Welfare.
The developer tried to show contrast . . . how the second organization structure would be an improvement over the first.

Of course, the words and figures, as reduced, are too small to
read. But can you imagine any reader being able to see where all
the various lines go and what the chart really means? In the "before" (the top chart), if the seven major units shown across the
top line had been shown on one chart, and the other charts
peeled off from it, possibly the reader could make some sense
out of it. When President Ford saw these charts, he dubbed
them "mess charts."

The developer of those complex charts did try to do a job.
The charts were well worked over. We understand that the proposed organization structure change was revised eight times before government executives and members of congress considered it finished.

If the developer doesn't use charting standards, the chart is
likely to be a mishmash of people, titles, and work. Most people

Government Simplification Department

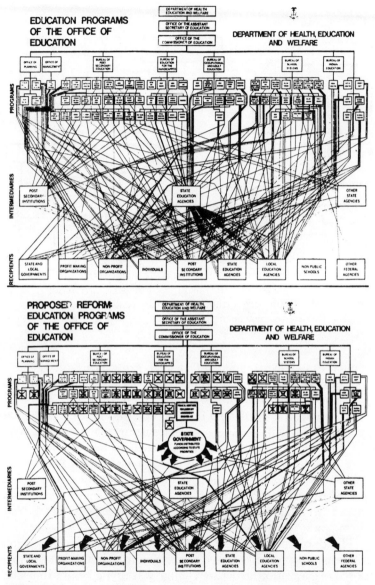

When a chart tries to show too much, it shows nothing. The developer used no standard "language" so these charts would just confuse the reader. People who need to know who does what and where, would turn their backs on such confusing charts.

who read charts don't have the time to think about the quality of a chart and whether the developer used a standard "language."

However, if you *are* the developer, you must take that time. A mishmash chart will have a name prominent in one box, a title prominent in the next, a work package name in another box, and finally a geographical designation.

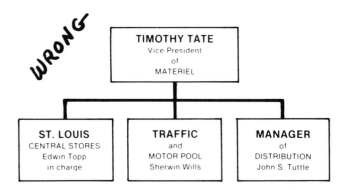

The low quality chart is a mish-mash. To achieve charting quality emphasize only one item ... THE WORK. Place the "work word" near the top of the box, in bold-face capitals. De-emphasize department names, job titles, individual names, geographical locations, and department numbers.

The activity of charting the organization received a deserved blow when Robert Townsend, in his book *Up the Organization*, equated organization charts with rigor mortis. Mr. Townsend was probably influenced by the poor quality of the charts he saw in the Avis Company. He recommends circular charts with people shown around one big table. These have been tried. They are stimulating, but we've never seen any such circular charts used consistently.

Numerous executives who read Townsend's book agreed with him. Why shouldn't they? They also have seen nothing but mishmash charts or overcrowded charts and they saw no value in them.

3. WHAT AN ORGANIZATION CHART CANNOT SHOW

An organization chart cannot show the personalities of the current holders of the positions shown on the chart. It cannot reveal strong characters and weak characters. The chart cannot show the inside politics and the power plays within the organization. Sure, they do exist, but how could you depict them? One person in a subordinate position may be more loyal to an executive in an entirely different group than the one to whom he reports. How do you show that on a chart?

The chart cannot explain the personal relationships between two executives that are happy or unhappy with each other. It cannot distinguish between newly appointed executives and the "old time" managers and executives. It can't show people's competence or incompetence.

An organization chart cannot reveal an untruthful or fictitious relationship. If the developer of the chart shows a fact that is not a fact, it is the developer who is a liar, not the chart. The chart is only a communication tool.

An organization chart cannot show the major *lateral* relationships that we call systems. It cannot do the same job that people's common eyeball-to-eyeball contacts do every day.

Some people say that we should not have organization charts. Undoubtedly this is because they have been disappointed in the poor quality of most charts. Also they may have expected a chart to do what no document could do. To say that we should not have an organization chart because it cannot show some things is like saying that because with a hammer you cannot saw wood or drill holes you will not use a hammer.

Remember what the chart is: *a mental tool.* Any tool has its limitations. But a tool can have value in its place and when people use it for its purpose. A tool cannot serve beyond its capability. To expect it to do so is foolish.

 Develop your chart to the very boundaries of its limitations but don't try to make it go beyond those limitations.

If you show too much on one chart, for example, the chart will simply confuse your reader. The quality chart, the useful one, is simple and its "picture" is very clear.

One executive may be strong in the organization because of his personal relationships with the president. Other men and women are just strong personalities. One woman may be very ambitious . . . and a peer of hers who is on the same hierarchical level is not ambitious at all. One man may have a blood relative who dominates the board of directors. A woman executive can be strong because of the amount of voting stock she or her family holds. Still another character shown on the chart could have a stronger influence than normal because he is "in solid" with an important customer.

4. WHAT A CHART CAN SHOW

A quality organization chart is one that is useful to anyone who needs to use it. It shows the organization structure and the work responsibility breakdowns as they actually exist. The chart reveals who reports to whom. It reveals the "division of work" that people perform in each of the organization's sub-units.

Does your own organization have five major structural parts, representing groups in such work specialties as accounting, selling, buying, engineering, and producing? Selling? Buying? Producing? What do those words represent? Work? Of course! And naming the *work* that groups of people do is the key to a quality chart.

 Work is basic. Work terms are the keys to a useful chart.

That's why the first caption you show in a box on the chart is the *work* that a group is expected to do.

Do not put the management titles in a prominent position, such as vice-president, chief, manager, director, or supervisor. Neither should you stress the name of the current occupant of a position such as Robert Smith or Barbara Moore. Occupants are temporary. They change. The work responsibility of the group is much more permanent.

So in each box you emphasize work. How? By naming the work in bold letters and then by putting that word near the top of the box, above people's names and their titles. Surround the work word with white space.

In addition to the boxes that depict specific "work packages," the quality chart shows how these work packages relate to each other in the "reporting to" sequences. That is true if the developer uses a meaningful pattern of connecting lines to indicate the hierarchical relationships. The relationships are vertical, not horizontal, as they are within a procedure. Important lateral relationships cannot be shown on a chart. Accept that limitation.

Each major sub-unit, such as the marketing department, has a number of sub-sub-units within it. Together these form a sort of pyramidal stack.

Let me explain. The lines connect the box depicting MARKETING with its sub-units such as SALES, MARKET RESEARCH, FORECASTING, and ADVERTISING. The connecting lines show what sub-units (work packages) are a part of the big work specialty of MARKETING. But those lines on the chart will not show how marketing people work as a team with the production people. That is the job of the procedure (the written document that reflects the systems channel).

In terms of personal relationships (between every two persons shown on the chart) the lines that connect the stack of boxes depict a two-way flow:

1. Downward *delegation*.
2. Upward *responsibility*.

If you search, you can find a few such quality charts. If you examine them closely, you will find that such charts really are a composite and show four pictures, including:

1. Name of the work package.
2. The official position titles.
3. The manager who is currently in charge.
4. The lines of delegation (downward) and the lines of responsibility (upward).

Think of the connecting lines between or among the boxes as a divided highway, with a two-way traffic flow. Delegated authority moves downward from a superior's box to the subordinate's box. There is also a flow of upward responsibility from each subordinate . . . up to the superior.

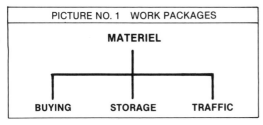

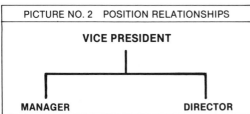

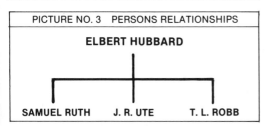

The quality organization chart shows four pictures. The first picture stresses the *work* of each segment. Picture No. 2 shows position relationships. Picture No. 3 shows personal relationships. (by itself this would be a staffing pattern, not a true organization chart because the work term is missing.) In Picture No. 4, the heaviest lines depict delegation and responsibility. (The dotted lines, shown here to help illustrate the 4th picture, are not actually used on a chart. Neither are the arrows.) Use just one thick line to connect the boxes.

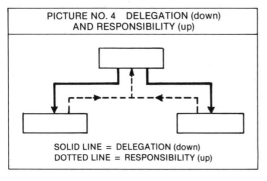

These lines, always drawn the same way, are to be a part of your organization chart's standard language* that your readers will learn to read. Those four pictures are just a few of the things that a quality chart can show.

5. HOW TO DEVELOP QUALITY CHARTS

Behind any quality chart are standards . . . standards for the boxes and the lines, the positions . . . and a standard position for the titles.

Make sure that your standards, as a set of guides, distinguish between the individuals shown on the chart and the groups that they head. EXAMPLE: A department is, of course, a group of people. The department's manager is an individual. On some charts the box represents the manager's work, not the group's work.

Use individual titles** consistently. Consider the term *manager*. Those who confer such a title on someone else need guidance. Exactly what is a "manager"? Is it the same as a "supervisor"? The organization's standards can explain, for example, that a manager is a person who *supervises* supervisors. In some cases organizations use the term "general supervisor" as a synonym for *manager*. Are they equivalent? Or does the general supervisor fit in somewhere between supervisor and manager?

Among some of the sillier things that we see on charts is a manager reporting to a manager who reports to a manager. These flaws would be eliminated if people just thought out what position titles really mean.

The term *supervisor* means someone who supervises the workers, someone who directs the rank-and-file employees. Then a *manager* is someone who supervises the supervisors. A vice-president is usually someone who has from two to ten managers reporting to him or to her. Seldom will vice-presidents have supervisors reporting directly to them.

Another aspect of the charting standards is the layout. Where do the specific boxes go? If one work group is the key group, if it represents the organization's "big show," how should you depict this fact . . . that it IS the key work group?

*This standard charting language which we will explain in this chapter is necessary for all charting . . . corporate, department, section, or group.
**Refer to the chapter on "Titles."

Do emphasize the work box that represents the organization's "big show." Briefly the "big show" is the major work package that you are showing on a specific chart. In the corporate (basic chart) the big show is the sub-unit around which the entire organization tends to pivot.

EXAMPLE: In a typical corporate chart, the big show work may be MARKETING. That is, all other functions will tend to support or to pivot around the activity covered by the work title of MARKETING.

As you produce peel-off charts that depict individual departments, they, too, will each have an individual "big show." This big show work is the department's major work. Every other activity in that department must pivot around and must support the big show activities. Depict this big show concept (and actuality) in the layout of the chart by placing it in the center.

After some thought your executives may consider that SALES is the big show of MARKETING. Therefore ADVERTISING, MARKET RESEARCH, and PROMOTION should be organized to support SALES. This can be shown on the chart by the position of the SALES box. Place it in the first row and center it.

In another major sub-unit (ADMINISTRATION) its sub-sub-unit could be the SYSTEMS AND COMPUTING section. Those words, "Systems and Computing" will show in the key box. In this peel-off chart there is also a "big show" activity, in this case SYSTEMS ANALYSIS. The box representing that activity is in the first row and is centered.

In tracing the hierarchical relationship upward, the director of SYSTEMS ANALYSIS reports to the vice-president of SYSTEMS AND COMPUTING, who in turn reports to a senior vice-president who rules ADMINISTRATION.

Boyd T. Mallory, the person in charge of Systems and Computing determined that the "big show" of his operation was SYSTEMS ANALYSIS. So that box appears in the center of the first line, Mr. Mallory himself is shown in the key box.

The key position is the "work package" that you are breaking up into its components. The chart is a "picture" of the way the key work breaks down into the work done by sections or groups. On each organization chart there will be one key box and at least one "big show" package of work. Show these by position. Sometimes there may be two "big shows."

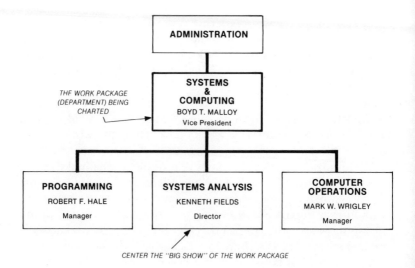

In this peel-off chart, SYSTEMS and COMPUTING is being charted. The "big show" of this sub-unit is SYSTEMS ANALYSIS. It is in a box that is centered and directly under the key box.

There is always a "big show" in each sub-unit of work. By getting people to think about this concept, the person in charge will tend to arrange the other units so that they support that "big show."

6. EMPHASIZE THE WORK

We don't have people in the organization just to carry titles or to hold posts or positions. They're all there *to work!* It is their work that makes the organization go. If no one works, the organization will die. So stress work in your charts. Prominent work titles are a part of your charting standards.

In a low-quality chart, a mishmash chart, the developer emphasizes the work one time, somebody's title in the next block, and then the occupant's name gets top billing. Another emphasis may be on the location such as the CHICAGO OFFICE.

That's wrong. Chart the work first. Emphasize the name of the work. De-emphasize management people, their titles, or geographical locations.

7. WHAT GOES IN THE BOX?

Even in the corporate chart (and in the key box that contains the name of the chief executive officer) do not emphasize either the title (president) or the man's name (Joel C. Reston). The work of the chief executive officer is MANAGEMENT ... or GENERAL MANAGEMENT ... or CORPORATE MANAGEMENT.

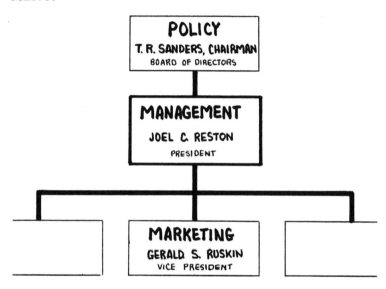

Emphasize the work. Include in each box the name of the work (use bold letters). Then show the current occupant of the position, and finally the occupant's official title.

A person's name, or the title of his or her job, is not work. Those are the secondary pictures provided by the chart. *Emphasize the work!* You do it in three ways. First, select the work title that really tells what the work is. Second, stress the work by the position of the work words ... at the top of the box. Thirdly, use a large, bold typeface for the work words. Incidentally, it is not necessary to set type for the chart captions. Legible hand-printing can serve, but do follow the caption standards.

In the three boxes above is a chart arranged the way it should be set up. In the past some stockholders of a corporation were shown on the top, but that is more fiction than fact. If there are any broad policies to be developed, they are generally developed by the board of directors under the direction of the chairman. For that reason we have depicted the board of directors block at the top. T. R. Sanders is the chairman of the board of directors. So he has an executive role to perform.

The significant charting of this corporation starts with the corporate key box. The title there is MANAGEMENT. The first breakouts on this corporate chart will include the major departments. Those are generally presided over by work specialists called vice-presidents. Such departments may include finance, engineering, production, marketing, personnel, and administrative services.

In this picture we show only one box below the management box, that of MARKETING. From its position, centered right under the key box, the charting language says that MARKETING is the "big show." Always locate the "big show" activity in the center of the chart right below the key box, in this case MANAGEMENT. Make all work titles dominate the chart:

Management . . . Marketing . . . Production
. . . Finance . . . Engineering . . . Personnel . . . Materiel

Such titles suggest the work that the organization's departments do. As we will see later, it is the "statement of work" that spells out more exactly what work is included under the work terms shown on the chart. The work title on the chart just starts the process of communication.

The reader, for example, is likely to want to know exactly what marketing work includes. You can almost guess if you have been around an organization very long. The activity would probably include the sales offices, promotion, forecasting of sales, advertising, and market research.

A fourth element in the box could be the department or section number. If such a number has been assigned, show it in the upper right-hand corner of the box.

Each segment of the organization has work to do. The people are there, in that segment, because your organization needs their help. They get results for the organization through the work that they do. The poor quality charts that you see so often do not stress work. On such charts the work descriptions are rather incidental . . . here and there. That's a mistake.

People in the organization *are* interested in knowing what work each department, each section, or each group does. Senior management wants to know. Department managers want to know what other departments do. Auditors want to know. Systems analysts want to know it so they can plan their systems and so that responsibilities assigned in the system are not contrary to the work already assigned to the various groups of people. Data processing people want to know. Outside consultants want to know who does what work and where they're located. Bankers and other financial people who do business with your organization want to know. So do some government agencies. Certainly most employees are interested in knowing *who* does *what* and *where* within their organization.

Let's repeat. Place the work word near the top of the box and in boldface type. The person's name, who is currently responsible for that work, can go on the next line. Set it in a smaller type. Remember that people are temporary. Finally, give the title of that person and letter it the smallest of the three. This is the order:

1. **WORK**
2. CURRENT OCCUPANT
3. Functional Title

Here is the way such a work package box will look:

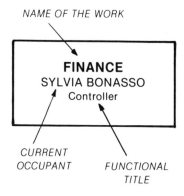

Harking back to the previous chart segment, would MAR-KETING include field services? Or customer services (complaints)? Does it include both domestic and foreign sales? If the sales are made in various ways, does marketing include direct mail? Do marketing people set up agencies or factory representatives?

These questions cannot be answered on the chart alone. If you put all of that information on the chart, then you'd have a statement of work, not a chart.

Rule: Use one document for only one specific purpose.

Hold your work titles (words that go in the boxes) down to one word if possible . . . certainly not more than two or three words. Select each work term carefully. (The words we put in the boxes are referred to as "captions.")

Are you composing the chart with a typewriter? If so, use capital letters and "letterspace" them for the *work word.* Letter space means that the typist leaves one extra space between each capital letter and two extra spaces between each word. EXAMPLE:

P R O M O T I O N & A D V E R T I S I N G

Leave two lines blank, then type the occupant's name in regular capital letters, like this:

ELLEN G. ANDERSON

Finally type the position title in "caps and lower case" letters, like this:

Vice- President

Put these captions in the rectangular box so that some white space flows *around* each caption. Don't jam them right up against the top line or have them sitting on the bottom line of the box.

Do consider hand lettering your charts. Find someone who has lettering skill and can handle black India ink.

What are the *earmarks* of a good organization chart? It is a chart that shows each basic work responsibility of the organization or of a single department. It uses work terms that any read-er can understand.

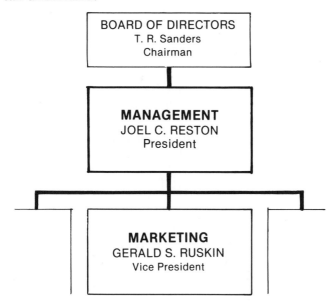

8. LAYING OUT YOUR CHART

Put your organization chart on a sheet of paper 8½ inches × 11 inches. Since the reader will insert it in a manual, arrange the layout for reading the 11-inch way . . . on the horizontal. The reader then turns the manual sideways.

The professional chart will "look good" to the reader. Even before he reads it, he has a "good feeling" about it because it is an attractive document.

On the sheet provide a ¾-inch white space all the way around . . . top, bottom, and sides. *No enclosing printed borders.* The white space frame is sufficient. The ¾-inch space at the top of the chart (on the 11-inch side) will be used for punching the holes for the binder rings.

Use a standard position for the document title. Call it what it is: ORGANIZATION CHART. We've used the upper right-hand corner for such a title block. You may prefer the left, since people start reading at the left. The block itself can be enclosed with printed rules.

Will this be the basic (corporate chart) or a departmental chart? If it is a department chart, tell what department or what section this chart represents. It is your policy to show an authorizing signature? Place it under the department's name. The executive to whom the person in the key box reports is the person who approves the chart.

Another item you'll need in the title block is the issue date or the revision date. Do you number your organizational units? Also show that number in this title block.

The chart, like your organization's letterhead, is a document that reflects the character of the organization. Important visitors, customers, or clients will see your organization charts.

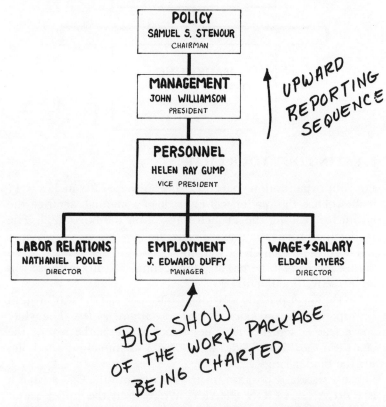

In this department chart explaining the work of PERSONNEL, the work of each of the department's major sub-units is depicted.

QUESTION: How many functional boxes should you show on a single 11″ × 8½″ chart? ANSWER: From six to 13. It is possible to lay out as many as 18 standard boxes on a normal typewriter sheet of paper (11″ × 8½″). But you'd be crowding the space, making the chart less attractive and therefore less readable. Use the peel-off technique (explained later).

9. ESSENTIALS OF A GOOD LAYOUT

To be useful to all readers the quality organization chart requires these layout essentials:

1. It is not crowded. The "picture" of the structure is clear.

2. There is one clearly indicated *key* box. It is centered and the chart is designed to show the break-outs from the key activity.

3. There are a limited number of break-out boxes, usually not more than 12.

4. One or two boxes are shown above the key box to explain the upward reporting sequence.

5. Each box has an accurate, meaningful *work* title. It is the most prominent caption.

6. Each executive's name is shown in somewhat smaller type.

7. The official job title is shown at the bottom of the box in subdued type.

8. It carries an effective date or a revision date.

9. There is a department number, if one is assigned.

10. It shows the official department name.

11. It has the approval signature of the key executive's superior.

You have probably seen one of those mammoth charts on some executive's office wall, displaying dozens of boxes or even including the names of every employee in the department. Naturally there is only one copy. Distribution to other people in a three-foot by five-foot format is not practical. Such a chart is hard to maintain, so in a few months it will fail to reflect the correct structure of the department. Do not take on the responsibility for such a chart. Let the department people do it, if they wish.

10. CHARTING STANDARDS

Your company's charts will communicate best if you select and then use a consistent charting "language." We recommend these 14 charting standards:

1. Provide standard sizes and line weights for the rectangular boxes. Give other people, who want to develop detailed charts, exact examples of these boxes and lines. Hold the number of box sizes down to four or five.

2. On each chart show the key position. Emphasize that position by using a medium width of line for the box. Place the work term represented by that box in the top center. *Example:* If you're charting the Materiel Division, the key box will be labeled MATERIEL. Sub-units such as BUYING, STOREROOMS, and RECEIVING will be in boxes on the next row down.

3. Show the upper sequence of command (above the key position you are now charting). Use smaller boxes. They are just as wide as other boxes, but are usually not as high, such as ⅝ inch in height.

4. Choose a meaningful word that will represent each specific work package. Two words may be required. Emphasize the work in each box.

5. To show a key staff position, use a small box. Place it to one side of the key box, *not* in the line.

6. To show the current executive's name, use the

first and last name. Do not use only initials unless the individual insists upon it.

7. In showing the functional title of the occupant of the box, use his or her *official* title. Secure a copy of the job description for that position from Personnel. It will carry the official title.

8. If you show department and section numbers (handy for auditors, accountants, and other staff people), place these numbers in the upper right-hand corner of each box. Also show the basic department number in the title block which is placed in an upper corner.

9. Place your chart on an 11″ × 8½″ white paper. Use 60 pound white book or 24 pound white bond. Specify a quality paper such as No. 2 sulphite. Punch the paper along the 11″ side, at the top of the chart, for insertion in the reader's manual.

10. For making up the two types of boxes and the connecting lines, specify three thicknesses of lines. Use the thickest of the three standard lines to *connect* the work units. These depict the downward delegation and the upward responsibility (the two-way street).

11. Do not show every employee on the *official* charts. If an individual supervisor develops a special subchart, then he can show his entire staff. But on the 10 or 12 official charts which you will develop, issue, and maintain, do not show all employees.

12. Date the chart. This will either be the effective date or the date of the revision.

13. If you decide to have an authorizing signature, place it in a standard position within the title block. *You do not* sign the chart. Neither does the person whose work package is being charted. The signer is the executive to whom the person in the key box reports.

14. Use a title block. Place it in the upper-right or
     left-hand corner of the sheet. There it will not
     take away space from the chart itself. Label the
     document ORGANIZATION CHART. Next
     name the division, department, or section being
     charted. The authorizing signature, the effec-
     tive date, and the department number (if any)
     are all enclosed in the title block.

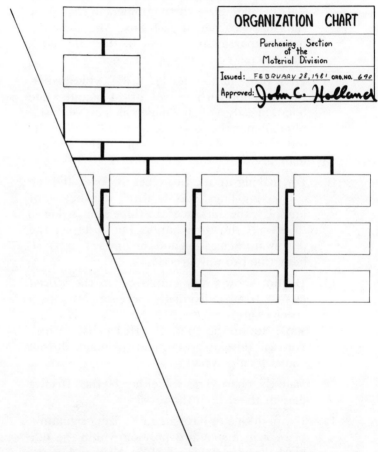

A neat title block for the chart can include the name of the document
(organization chart), the division and the section being charted. The
block can include the approval signature, the issue date and the organization number, if any.

11. BUILDING BLOCKS OF THE CHART

The purpose of an organization chart is to provide readers, who have a need to know, with a picture of the organization's working structure. The reader wants to know how many work activities there are, how they are grouped, and how they relate to each other. To develop a meaningful chart start with a few simple *visual* elements. Building blocks of a useful chart consist of the following:

1. Three sizes of rectangular boxes.
2. Three widths of inked lines.
3. Standard positions for the three caption words that go in the boxes.

Do standardize on a relatively few visual devices so that your chart will be easy to read. Do not use a heterogeneous array of boxes and lines of all widths. Be cautious about *any* use of a dotted line. We advise against its use. The dotted line has been the most confusing element of the thousands of charts we've seen.

Use the three line widths for specific purposes. The lightest line (hairline) will be used for most boxes. Use the *medium* line only for the key box . . . the box that represents the work being charted. Use the heaviest line only to show the connections between the boxes. These heavy lines represent such intangibles as delegation, authority, and responsibility.

The standard boxes will be 1¾ inches wide and ⅞ inch high. Boxes used to show upward reporting and staff functions will be the same width (1¾ inches) but will be only ⅝ inch high.

If your reproduction equipment for making charts requires it, the boxes could be somewhat higher or wider. However, the boxes presented here have been satisfactory for use on hundreds of quality charts. The specified widths will allow you to string five boxes on one horizontal line. The box and line standards are on the next page.

The weight (thickness) of the line is a part of the charting language. Let us repeat. Reserve the heaviest line (to use a printer's terms, 1½ points) to connect the boxes and to depict such intangible flows as delegation, responsibility, and accountability.

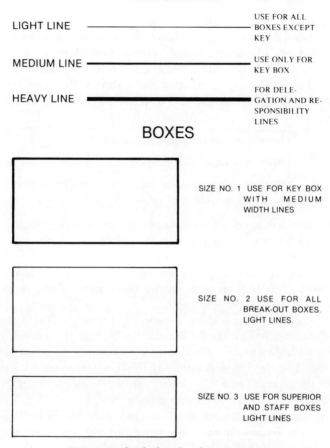

LINE WIDTHS

LIGHT LINE ———————————— USE FOR ALL BOXES EXCEPT KEY

MEDIUM LINE ———————————— USE ONLY FOR KEY BOX

HEAVY LINE ▬▬▬▬▬▬▬▬▬ FOR DELE-GATION AND RE-SPONSIBILITY LINES

BOXES

SIZE NO. 1 USE FOR KEY BOX WITH MEDIUM WIDTH LINES

SIZE NO. 2 USE FOR ALL BREAK-OUT BOXES. LIGHT LINES.

SIZE NO. 3 USE FOR SUPERIOR AND STAFF BOXES LIGHT LINES

Your standard charting language can include three widths of lines and as few as two sizes of boxes. The medium weight line is reserved for use on the key box. All other boxes are made up of a very light line (hairline).

Now let's look at some chart arrangements. The first one illustrates a wrong and right way to show the breakout boxes.

In the top layout notice the string of four breakout boxes (A, B, C, and D) and the heavy lines that run downward. No doubt the second row of boxes (E. F, G, and H) shows a reporting sequence upward to the box in the first row. But does box I show a reporting sequence to E? Or to A? Arranged that way, the layout language isn't clear.

Now look at the second (lower) layout. Here the language is clear. The second and third row of boxes represent a reporting responsibility to the first row. Where there is more than one subunit reporting, run the heavy line along the side of the boxes.

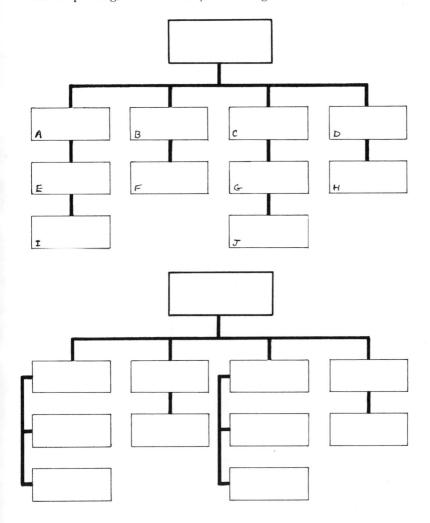

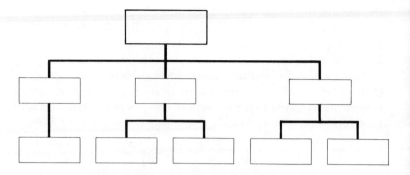

In the above layout the language is clear. The "big show" box is centered and the reporting sequences of the sub-sub-units are apparent.

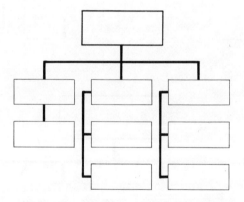

Above is another chart layout in which the language is clear. The "big show" work is centered and the reporting sequences of the sub-sub-units are clear.

In the following layout the big show work is not clear. However, the reporting sequences are. Every sub-unit reports directly to the executive in the key box.

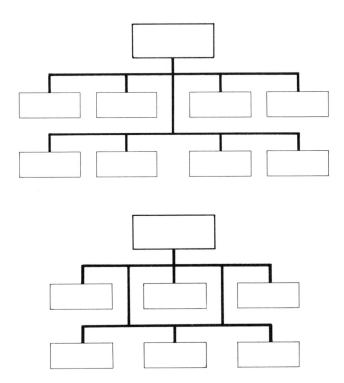

In the above layout the big show box is clear. Again all sub-units are shown as reporting directly to the executive occupying the key box.

The organization structure is made up of both line and staff functions. To depict staff functions (off line) show them on either side of the key box, like this:

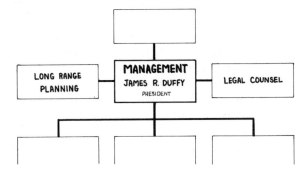

LONG RANGE
PLANNING

MANAGEMENT
JAMES R. DUFFY
PRESIDENT

LEGAL COUNSEL

12. HOW MANY CHARTS?

Don't go overboard on the quantity of your *official* charts. Develop only enough charts to depict the major facets of your organization's working structure. THEN STOP! Do not issue more than 12 to 16 charts. Do not show every employee on any chart. If you don't hold back you'll run into two problems:

1. Your charts can become so detailed that the basic work structure pattern will appear fuzzy.
2. You won't be able to keep numerous charts up to date.

EXAMPLE: The people in one large organization (18,000 employees) discovered the value of standardizing the "language" on their charts. So far, so good.

But then some higher up decided that if a dozen charts were so useful many charts should be better. So overboard they went, developing a chart for every sub-sub-sub-unit. Soon they had issued over 300 charts. Technically the charts were well done . . . accurate and attractive. They used tons of paper. Within a year five people were working steadily preparing or revising those charts. At the "production" peak they had 317 different charts. You can guess what finally happened.

The many charts were not maintained because the changes were too frequent. One woman executive said, "I won't change the chart now because there'll be other changes in a week or two." Then along came an economy wave and those same 317 charts (which should be as up to date as any document in the organization) quickly became obsolete. And *useless*. The charts no longer reflected the organization's structure.

ADVICE: Issue relatively few charts but revise them, if there are minor changes, every three months. If a major change takes place, revise the chart at once.

It may be ideal to reissue a chart after each change, but plain old money economics will dictate otherwise. So set up a method for picking up all the minor changes, accumulating them, and reissuing the chart every 90 days.

How many charts should you develop to reflect your major sub-units?

EXAMPLE: Consider a medium-sized manufacturing organization of 2400 employees. The charts will include one corporate chart, reflecting the over all responsibility of the chief executive officer (MANAGEMENT). Then seven peel-off charts reflect the work of the seven departments. These are directed by second-line major executives (vice-presidents). These men and women direct the functions of MARKETING, ACCOUNTING AND FINANCE, PRODUCTION, ADMINISTRATION, ENGINEERING, PERSONNEL, and MATERIEL.

In that example, the chart developer provided only eight charts. The single corporate chart gave people the overview, then each of the work packages (directed by each of the seven vice-presidents) was represented on the corporate (basic) chart. Charts that reflect those seven departments were "peel-offs" from the corporate chart.

The corporate chart showed the president's staff support in boxes that were on the left and right of the MANAGEMENT box. The "big show" department (Production) issued five section charts. However, these were not maintained by the corporate documents officer.

Be careful to distinguish between an *assistant position* and an *assistant to* position. An assistant TO the president is a staff worker and is "off line." An assistant president is in the line and could give orders to the vice-presidents.

An assistant *to* the president, who is also the chief of corporate staff (a heavyweight), can be shown in a staff position. Four or five staff boxes may be required. Whether they're on the right or left is of no significance.

In a large organization with numerous subsidiaries the staff functions can be sizeable. If the president has a chief of staff with numerous support staff people reporting to him or her, a peeled-off staff chart can be developed.

If the functions of all subsidiaries require corporate guidance in such key functions as FINANCE, PUBLIC RELATIONS and RESEARCH, the corporate chart could look like the full chart shown on the following page.

Do not show staff functions reporting to the vice-presidents on the corporate chart. Do show any such secondary staff positions on the seven departmental "peel-off" charts.

If you issued only from 8 to 12 charts, even though changes

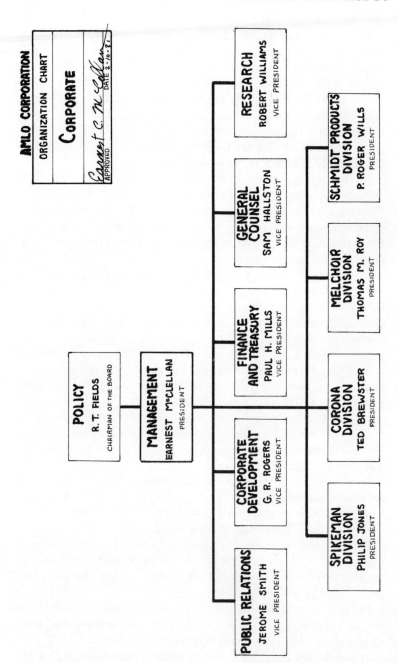

are frequent you can maintain them. That is, you could maintain them if you use simple inexpensive methods for such maintenance. If the department managers want further peel-offs for their sections, suggest that they produce and maintain their own charts.

Do provide the department's chart developer with your "standard charting language." This will be your company's official charting language. Then any subcharts will appear to be related to the corporate chart and to the department charts. All will have a "family appearance."

Do you show department numbers in the blocks on the major charts? If so, then the standards will call for related numbering. EXAMPLE: If the PRODUCTION department is 200, MANUFACTURING CONTROL could be 201, STOCKROOMS 202, INDUSTRIAL ENGINEERING 203, etc.

13. PEEL OFF THE SECONDARY CHARTS

To insure that each chart provides a clear picture, do not try to show too much on one chart. Rather use the peel-off technique.

On the basic (corporate) chart show only the major functions such as MARKETING and PRODUCTION. However, include all functions in which the executives in charge report directly to the president. This chart will include the corporate "big show" (or shows—there could be two) and the major support activities such as ACCOUNTING or PERSONNEL.

O.K. On the corporate chart let's say that you show MARKETING as a major department and indicate that it is the big show of your firm.

What work is included in MARKETING? To show that detail, produce a departmental chart. Now the key box will be labeled MARKETING. The breakout boxes may include SALES, PROMOTION, MARKET RESEARCH, FORECASTING, and ADVERTISING. Let's say that in your company ADVERTISING is the marketing department's big show. Place the ADVERTISING box right under the key box. Urge people to carry the big show concept right on down the hierarchy. This helps each manager and each supervisor to think about the relative importance of their activities.

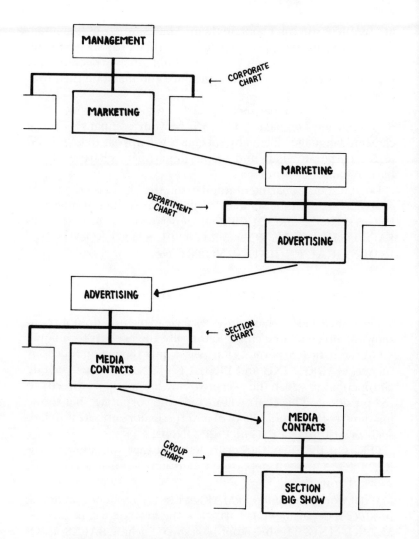

By using the peel-off technique you avoid crowding
the chart. If needed, other people can provide useful
charts for any number of hierarchical "layers" without crowding any one chart.

Carry the official charting only to the secondary level. Other
people, if they want further breakdown charts, can continue to

use the peel-off technique. This peel-off technique is a part of your charting standards. Thus if you showed only seven major work packages on the corporate chart, you'd develop only seven separate charts for each of these major work packages.

14. AN INDIVIDUALIZED CHART

Work packages cost money. Some executives have enjoyed specialized (custom made) charts showing expenses on the chart. Of course, these figures are not published. They are just added to one executive's chart.

Other added figures can include staff size, or total salaries, or total equipment investment.

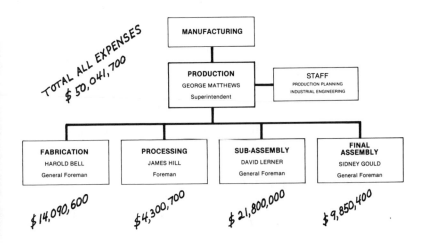

15. WHO DECIDES ON THE ORGANIZATION STRUCTURE?

Let's make this clear: the chart developer does *not* decide on the corporate structure. Only top executives do. Thus the developer serves strictly as (1) a staff adviser on management documentation and (2) as a guide to the most effective charting techniques.

Usually the work of planning the organization structure oc-
curs in fits and starts. When a new chief takes over, everything
changes. Obviously the chief executive officer determines the
best arrangement of the corporation's work packages. Deciding
on the structural working arrangement is truly an executive decision and each chart is a reflection of that decision.

16. THE CHART'S SISTER DOCUMENT—THE STATEMENT OF WORK

Your set of organization charts developed as a real tool for management's thinking and for communication provides clear views
of all of the work activity in the organization. It tells, briefly, who
has what responsibility for doing what work. Carefully chosen
"work words" in the boxes help the reader.

Yet the chart's work terms can only start the process of "shed-
ding light" on what all the people do. Like a series of strobe
flashes, the chart gives an overview on the subject of work and
the people who do that work.

To turn the big floodlight on the organization's work, a com-
panion document is necessary . . . a *statement of work*. The brief-
est way to explain this related document is that it is a department's "job description."

17. LATERAL RELATIONSHIPS

The chart explains the structure of the various groups in terms
of the work that each group does. It explains the reporting sequences, reveals the chain of command, and how the various
work specialties relate. It answers such questions as "How does
advertising relate to *sales*?" or "How does *shipping* relate to *ware-
housing*?" Most of those are vertical relationships, the up the ladder and down the ladder chain of command.

But how about showing the lateral relationships that exist *between* and *among* the work specialties? The chart doesn't show
these.

EXAMPLE: How does the work of ACCOUNTING connect with
the activity of PURCHASING? What is the relationship between
engineering and outside manufacturing?

There is only one document that can make such relationships clear and it is the *procedure*. But most procedures, like the average management document, are poor. They are not good tools to manage by. So we will present one procedure development that is a good tool of management . . . *Playscript*. Glance at an organization chart. In looking at any work-specialty pyramid, you may think:

> The total work of this organization has been broken down into logical subpackages of work. Every group of work specialists is now shown in separate tiers or pyramids of boxes. QUESTION: What is the reason for the division of all the work? ANSWER: Because work specialists need to be guided (managed) by a person who knows that work specialty. Salesmen need a sales leader, a sales *manager*.

Yet all the work specialists are part of the organization. The company as a whole is still a single unit. Some means must be used to bring these broken-apart work segments back into a form of coordinated activity . . . into an action-getting system. Such lateral communication is essential if your firm is to achieve teamwork.

EXAMPLE: In a system called "purchasing," various specialty groups do play a role. There must be an effective "interface" among the various work specialists. People in the MATERIEL department will take part. So will the requestor who is in one of the operating departments. Another "actor" in this lateral activity can be someone in the stockroom. A buyer within the MATERIEL department plays the pivot role. Finally a man or woman in the receiving section will handle the purchased item when it arrives on your receiving dock.

Thus the lateral or teamwork document needs will be covered briefly in this book under the chapter titled PROCEDURES. Procedures are written explanations of the various systems. And by the way, systems are not computers: computers are systems tools.

Systems are plans for people to use in working together . . . thus providing for effective lateral communication . . . which enables people to get teamwork results.

Chapter 3

STATEMENTS OF WORK

If an executive, or anyone else, wants to know what people in a department do, a box on the organization chart can only start the informational process.

As a fair analogy, consider the taking of a photograph. The photographer's first exposure of the scene (through the lens of the camera) merely starts the picture-getting process. To be viewed clearly, the latent image on the film must be developed and printed.

The organization chart is like that first exposure. By contrast the statement of work is the development of that first "exposure" on the chart. However, if the picture (or chart) is not properly exposed, the subsequent full-blown picture will not be clear. This is why we urge: "Use well-known *work* words on the chart. Avoid euphemisms (high-sounding words for ordinary activities) on your charts."

1. CHARTS ALONE AREN'T ENOUGH

So to develop a clear picture of your organization's work patterns you use statements of work. The two documents, (1) charts and (2) statements of work, are closely related. To start the statement use exactly the same word that you used in the box on the chart, like MARKETING . . . ACCOUNTING . . . or ENGINEERING.

In a quality organization chart, the work term that you place in the box does provide a sort of "statement of work."

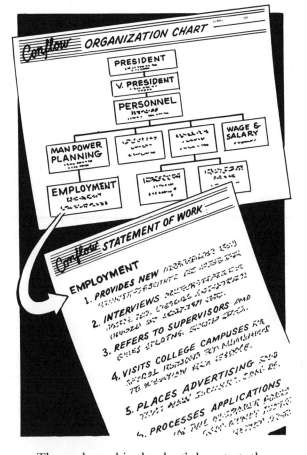

The work word in the chart's box starts the process of communicating. It is the statement of work that clarifies what the chart's work word really includes. In this illustration the statement spells out all the work that the EMPLOYMENT section does.

EXAMPLE: Consider the department titled SHIPPING. That word gives the reader a barely exposed "picture" of what the shipping department does.

Let's repeat: The chart's "work word" only starts the communication process. It is the *work statement* that continues on and spells out, in more useful detail, what the SHIPPING DEPARTMENT does. So those two documents . . .

1. *The Organization Chart*
2. *The Statement of Work*

. . . cannot be handled separately. When you develop one, or revise one, also look at the other. The two documents must always be closely connected, since they are the prime techniques for both planning and for communicating information about the organization.

Start the statement on the work with a summary. It may be only a sentence. Here is a series of such brief summaries used by a manufacturing company:

Department	*Statement of Work Summaries*
Manufacturing	Makes the company's products
Engineering	Designs the company's products
Sales	Sells the company's products
Quality Control	Assures that products are up to standard
Personnel	Provides the required human skills
Finance	Provides money and financial controls
Accounting	Reports on financial results
Materiel	Procures, stores, and furnishes all services, materials and supplies
Administration	Provides supporting services, including systems and data processing, mailroom operations, telephones, communications, library, motor pool, security, and the maintenance of grounds and buildings

These summary statements could be placed at the top of each department's statement of work. Consider the next-to-last summary . . . the one on MATERIEL. The department's chart started the process, using the term MATERIEL in the key box. The above summary expanded on that one word. So a typical statement would start with the same name of the work as on the

chart. After the statement provides an all-encompassing summary, it spells out (in reasonable detail) the work of each sub-unit.
EXAMPLE:

Statement of Work

MATERIEL

Major Function

Procures, stores, and furnishes all
services, materials and supplies

Detailed Functions

1. Ships and/or receives all items.
2. Maintains inventory controls and records.
3. Operates the material release system.
4. Arranges for and controls subcontracts on off-site manufacturing.
5. Procures all production and nonproduction materials and supplies.
6. Makes all vendor, services, or supplier contacts.
7. Stores and issues purchased parts and production materials.
8. Stores and furnishes semifinished goods.
9. Warehouses materials for parts as required, including parts or work-in-process items that must go off-line temporarily.
10. Operates the stationery stockroom.
11. Operates all production line stockrooms.
12. Operates truck and passenger automotive equipment in the motor pool.
13. Handles all traffic matters related to material movements to and from the plant and branch plants.
14. Provides travel and hotel reservations and all requirements for employees traveling on company business.
15. Forecasts material requirements, in conjunction with marketing personnel.
16. Crates and ships the products destined for overseas.
17. Provides specialized procurement personnel to serve the engineering experimental production facility.

On the related MATERIEL organization chart, only six breakout boxes appeared. Since the detailed work statements totaled 17, obviously some sections were responsible for the work described in two or three sentences.

It may appear that sentence 1 and sentence 16 were duplicates. But the work covered in sentence 16 requires special overseas packing and handling, so a separate group of seven people performed this work.

From an audit viewpoint sentence 1 raises a question of functional separation. Should RECEIVING be located in the same department that *ordered* the articles? On the recommendation of an internal auditor the receiving function was transferred to the department of ADMINISTRATION.

2. AN INVENTORY OF THE CURRENT WORK

Your organization may not have statements of work. They may exist under other titles such as "functional outlines" or "departmental responsibilities." If so, the first set of statements will be eye-openers for top managers.

In effect these documents will become work inventories of the present activities. Statements of work will reveal all the work and in which department it is performed. On the drafts, include the staff size required to do the job, along with the *total* yearly cost of doing that work. This will not be published but will be put in (by hand) on the copies of certain executives. Continuing with the MATERIEL department example, a sentence for the executives could look like this:

```
13.   Handles all traffic matters related to

      material movements to and from the

      plants and branch plants
```

STAFF OF 9
BUDGET $184K

Obtain the yearly costs and size of staff from the department heads. Include the figure on their final drafts. EXPLAIN: Those figures will not be published in the regular statements of work. Later they will be added (by hand) for a limited number of key executives, including the president.

So your first statements of work become an inventory of the work that hundreds, or even thousands of people are *now* doing. One immediate result is that the original statements will serve as a work inventory—by groups. They'll tell management exactly what each group is doing now . . . and how much it costs.

Upon receiving work information in such a useful form, executives tend to react immediately. They'll want to make changes in the current responsibilities and assignments.

So a dozen well-written statements of work are not just more paperwork. They are management *tools*! Statements of work carry information that is just as important as a corporation's charter. Many benefits will soon be clear.

Fifty years ago the average organization was relatively stable but that is not so today. The organization today is not so much a structure as it is a process.

Circumstances change. Markets change. Old products die; new products are born. Customers change. Suppliers change. Responsibilities shift. New regulations arrive. New competitors spring up.

New "professions" can emerge in three or four years; other skills and professions become obsolete. The human pivots—the supervisors and the managers—also change. Some are new, some old, some are tired, some retired. Some people grow. Some people shrink. Others just spin around in circles.

Every change requires some adjustment in the organization's structure. If the structure is not changed, the organization is soon limping along with a structure that was adequate for the needs of a period 20 years past. Change. Change. Change. Adjust! Adjust!

3. PURPOSES OF THE STATEMENT OF WORK

At certain time intervals, senior executives in the company must *reconsider* their organizational structure. If they feel that some activities should be curtailed, expanded, or combined, these executives can do so only if they have accurate, significant information about the work patterns of the present structure. Only then can company officers make sensible alterations. The process of thinking about the organizational structure needs factual inputs.

We've seen executives struggle with big, thick reports from outside consultants, trying to digest the thousands of words. Often such reports are not even read.

Executives couldn't get a better explanation of the organization than from an accurate work-word on the organizational chart and a related well-written statement of work. Thus both the charts and the statements are truly tools that executives use "to manage by."

In one large organization analysts identified more than 1,000 distinct types of work specialties that employees were then performing. Such work specialties need identification in one place ... on the charts and then spelled out, at least briefly, in the statements of work. Such activities cost millions of dollars.

Top executives aren't the only ones who need such tools. Staff people need them, too. Consider the situation where a senior analyst has been assigned to help improve the reports that come to the vice-president of the MATERIEL department. The vice-president receives 73 reports a month, some currently provided on demand on the video tube, others as "hard copy" computer print-outs. Couldn't that analyst do a better job if she was aware of the various types of work that the 242 persons in the MATERIEL department do?

Study the two documents together ... the chart and the statement of work. Any person who does study these documents will have a clear picture of the current organization structure and the work done by the people within that structure. The delegation and responsibility connections will be apparent.

Without such documents, no one, not even the president, can have a clear picture of the work activity in the organization. Rather it will be hazy, blurred, and indistinct.

Together the two documents, the organization chart and the statement of work, are powerful thinking aids for all people who have a need to know.

Study the two documents together. The work title on the chart starts the task of describing the department's work. Expand the description on the statements.

We must expect the organization itself to have a major goal. Then anyone can ask: "Does each work package, now functioning in the organization, lead toward that goal?"

Obviously the man (or woman) who develops management's documents must know what those goals are. If the statement of the goal is not published and distributed widely, the document developer can get a copy from the company's long-range planners. People involved in a management by objective (MBO) program will also know the goals.

Based on the corporation's specific goals, each department can then set sub-goals within its work specialty jurisdictions. Each of these sub-goals must be in harmony with the corporate goal. In turn, sub-groups *within* the department must have specific, attainable goals that are harmonious with both those of the department AND those of the corporation.

But here we have hundreds, even thousands of people at work. Does that tremendous quantity of work really boost the organization along toward its goals?

 Without management documents, who can tell?

If an executive knows the work of all the departments, then, based on such knowledge he can see whether each work activity is helping to achieve the corporation's goals. He can add up all the work statements and they will describe the total work of the entire organization.

4. VALUES FROM USING STATEMENTS OF WORK

We've mentioned some of the values. There are others. In almost any organization there is a considerable amount of *wheel-spinning.* These are activities that really do not contribute to the achievement of the organization's goals. Nor do they support other work that may be contributing.

Even worse, there is usually a percentage of the work that actually pulls the organization *away from achieving its goals!* Such work has a negative value. Some work can be of a parasitical nature, draining away the productive values of other work.

If they are really negative insofar as helping the organization to achieve its goals, how can such work activities exist? There are two reasons:

1. Work of negative value exists because people usually think primarily in terms of work that has been done in the past. They do not ask whether that work really helps the organization move toward its goals.

2. The executives do not have a composite view of all the organization's work.

So pin down all the work, good or bad. You start the revelation of what work is going on in your organization with a good organization chart. REMINDER: Stress that the chart must not emphasize geography, people, titles, or anything else. It must stress *work* . . . ONLY WORK!

Statements of work enable an executive to ask significant questions. Let's say that the chief executive officer (CEO), along with his vice-president of MATERIEL, is reviewing the latter's department. The CEO will want to know specifically what work the MATERIEL department does. The properly written statement of work will make it clear. The CEO may not have realized that this department handles *material release*. He may not even know what material release is, but at least now he can ask.

Auditors who study these statements of work may recommend that the functions of receiving should not be in MATERIEL because of the danger of employee-supplier collusion.

Since MATERIEL is a support and service activity, other men and women, in every department, will have an interest in what goes on in MATERIEL. Just how detailed should the information be? Do the statements provide all that the executive in charge of MATERIEL (the vice-president) needs to know?

How about the purchasing agent, the person in charge of all buying? Could he or she do a better job of managing if all the work done in MATERIEL was clearly stated?

The purchasing agent's subordinates deal routinely with every other department. Therefore, would a buyer be helped if he could see, quickly, what work each other department does?

How about the people who work in those other departments? Do they all realize the extent of the activities that their own department carries on? It is true that, over a long period of time, employees will find out about other activities. But why not speed up the process so everybody can be more effective sooner?

We do evaluate the performance of individuals. But how about the performance of groups, whether they are big departments or small units comprised of only two or three employees? Should their performance and productivity be evaluated? The statement of work can be a basis for such evaluation.

If, in a departmental statement of work, there are sixteen substatements, how many people does it take to carry out each of those subpackages of work? (At least one person must have the prime responsibility for the work reflected by one sentence.) How *well* are they doing that specific work? Do consider *quality* as well as the *quantity* of the work output.

But first ask the healthiest of questions: "Is that work necessary at all?" If no one ever asks that question, useless work can and sometimes does continue for a generation. Can you afford such waste?

There are other values to be gained from up-to-date charts and statements of work. Most firms use the services of consultants. These people all have an immediate *need to know* before they can plunge in to solve a problem. Otherwise the consultant must use days, weeks, or even months to find out who-does-what-and-where. (This author knows. He has been such a consultant and most places don't have these documents to help him get off to a fast start. Or what documentation they do furnish is either (1) obsolete or (2) of such poor quality that it is useless.)

How much does such a sloppy manner of using consultants waste in real money each year? Probably, across the continent, billions of dollars.

One of the biggest surprises is to find that some groups are doing work that executives *do not want them to do*. We have found some groups taking on work that had been previously assigned to another group. The originally assigned group may not have done the work or did it badly.

Clear statements of work can eliminate department boundary disputes or jurisdictional disputes between supervisors or foremen. When a supervisor *knows* what her subordinates are assigned to do, she need not question whether they are overstepping the bounds of her section's assigned responsibility.

Sure, there are many people who don't like to be pinned down on what their duties are. Also they don't want anyone to know how well they are doing their work. They much prefer to keep these duties vague and fuzzy, perhaps sending out "whitewash" reports that no one ever checks. Such people will not like to be required to use meaningful work words as titles on the chart. Neither will they like specific statements of work. So expect some opposition to any management document program from such people. They're most likely to call it "unnecessary paperwork."

5. AUTHORITY GOES WITH RESPONSIBILITY

Everybody knows that to carry out his or her responsibility, the person needs sufficient matching authority. If a man is responsible for painting a wall and its doors, he also has the authority to keep people away from those walls and doors until the paint dries. So he has the right to put up signs that say: KEEP OUT. WET PAINT.

Henri Fayol, the great French industrialist, developed and stated a basic, long-enduring list of "Rules of Organization." Anyone who violates those rules always comes to grief because they are so fundamental. One of these rules is the "unity of command." If two supervisors can give a single employee orders, chaos will ensue. Even the Bible warns us that "a man cannot serve two masters." The employee will be frustrated and confused. On the battlefield such a violation of this rule will lead to defeat.

Duplication of effort can soak up the organization's energy and resources. In some cases we have seen triplication of effort.

Authority is a rather vague concept. But it is an essential part of the management process, so we will consider later how to determine who has what responsibility and what authority.

Once a supervisor has been assigned a work duty, she is both *responsible* for carrying out that work and she must have the *authority* required.

6. A BASE FOR GOOD SYSTEMS

To be effective, every document used as a tool in the management process must be consistent with every other management tool or document. A chart cannot be inconsistent with a statement of work. A statement of work cannot refute a policy. A procedure must not run contrary to what is called for in a policy.

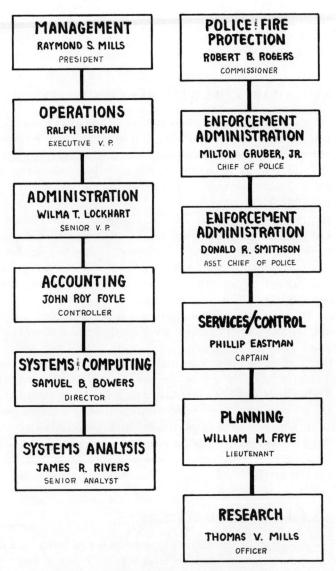

The exact chain of command stretches from chief executive officer to the operating worker. One person can report only to one superior. Thus the chain also provides for "unity of command."

Three management documents assign specific work to people, both to individuals and to groups. These are:

1. The organization chart
2. The statement of work
3. The procedure

Now a procedure is not a system. IT IS A WRITTEN DOCU-MENT THAT DESCRIBES A SYSTEM. The procedure tells who does what and in what sequence. It is a document that helps people to achieve *teamwork* results. Therefore the procedure's assignment of work includes what the computer does. The computer is, indeed, one of the "actors" in the systems drama.

In developing a system, the analyst "assigns" work responsibilities to various groups of people . . . to the work specialists. Thus the system is a device for coordination. Planned systems are absolutely essential if the organization is to get its big jobs done such as:

Manufacturing, designing, paying, collecting, selling, and supplying manpower.

The system as reflected by its covering procedure lines up the basic work assignments (as set forth in the organization charts and in the statements of work) into an action pattern. Here's an excerpt from one such pattern. It was used in a hospital:

PROCEDURE

Subject: Admitting a Patient

Performed By		**Actions**
Physician	1.	When hospitalization of a patient is required, notifies the admitting department and makes a reservation for patient.
Admitting Clerk	2.	Records the reservation and completes preadmission form 115C.

	3. Mails form 115C to patient.
Patient	4. Fills out upper portion of 115C as called for on the form itself.
	5. Mails completed form 115C back to hospital.
Admitting Clerk	6. Upon return of preadmission form:

6a. Checks bed records for available space and schedules the room and the required service.

6b. Asks Medical Records for any previous medical information on patient.

6c. Files form 115C alphabetically until patient is admitted.

Medical Record Clerk	7. Pulls patient's medical record, charges to and sends to Admitting.
Patient	8. On the scheduled day, applies to the Admissions Office.
Admitting Clerk	9. Retrieves preadmission form 115C, interviews patient and then completes the regular admitting form 119M.

10. If previous hospital service has been given, notes this previous admission on form 119M.

11. Obtains remaining information from patient or from responsible person.

12. Secures financial information.

12a. If there are any credit questions, refers them to the admitting officer.

13. Requests addressograph operator to make up identification plate for patient.

14. When plate is received, stamps all required forms pertaining to patient.

15. Telephones nursing station and requests an escort for patient.

16. In the meantime:

    16a. Distributes copies of form 119M to all departments involved.

    16b. Sends medical records to nursing station.

    16c. Notifies patient's doctor by telephone.

    16d. If needed, fills out insurance forms.

    16e. Files copy of admission form (119M) alphabetically until patient is ready for discharge.

Nursing Station

17. Sends aide for patient.

Aide

18. Takes patient to room, then notifies floor nurse that patient is now in room.

Nurse, assisted by Aide

19. Prepares patient for bed.

    19a. Fills out clothes list.

    19b. Lists valuables and places them in envelope and seals.

Nurse

20. Takes envelope to nursing office for placement in the Admitting Office safe.

That procedure is written in the "Playscript" format. We'll consider *Playscript* more fully in the chapter on procedures. The point here is that the procedure does reflect the admitting *system*. It does assign duties to people and groups of people, such as the nursing station. So each assignment of work duties in a procedure (and in a system) *must be consistent* with those assigned in charts and statements of work. Any inconsistency from document to document creates confusion.

Let us repeat: A procedure, written correctly, is a *reflection* of the system. The work assignments shown in the procedure must be consistent with the work responsibilities assigned in the statements of work.

The systems analyst, through his or her plan, weaves these management assigned duties into the data flow that gets results.

   It is the systems plan that lines up selected work sequences into a coordinated effort, into teamwork that moves big volumes of transactions through the various systems channels.

We have seen situations where the system (and its procedure) assigned duties and responsibilities to work groups that have *never been officially assigned these responsibilities.* Some of the people in the group were not qualified to do the work called for in the procedure.

In one example the company (an electronics manufacturer) thought it had a shortage of engineers. Soon PERSONNEL was hard at work finding engineers. We found that a procedure, written years before, had assigned non-engineering duties to engineers. These included proofing, copying bills of material, etc. We changed the procedure, assigning such duties to clerks, hired four clerks, and found the company really had a surplus of engineers. And the clerks did the work better.

7. INDIVIDUAL WORK

Use statements of work only to describe the work of employee groups . . . of divisions, departments, sections, units, bureaus. The duties of individual employees are documented in PERSONNEL'S *job descriptions.* Most people know about job descriptions. As we mentioned earlier, the statement of work is a "department's job description."

There is also a need for documents that spell out an individual's duties. These include job descriptions, task outlines, and work instructions. Top managers don't usually use these, but supervisors and personnel people do. The point here is that the documents describing a group's duties are different from those relating to an individual's performance. And we have developed document formats (task outlines) that do aid individuals. That is another subject.

A common mistake in a statement of work is to describe what a manager, as an individual, does when actually his or her group *does* it. The manager's responsibility isn't to do the work. It is to see that subordinates do it.

Make up your mind. Are you writing a statement of work or a job description or a task outline? The three are not the same. Don't mix them.

You say one supervisor (or manager) does some of the group's work personally? Then write the sentence that reflects this work as though he is a *part* of the group, not the supervisor.

It's only the work that groups do that concerns us here. Those are genuine *statements of work*. A manager is a single employee. You describe his personal work just as you do the work of any employee . . . with a job description or a task outline.

8. WRITING THE STATEMENT

Your writing job starts with the work word used in the block on the organization chart. Was that word carefully chosen? If so, you're on your way.

If the chart's work word is a euphemism or a title without a work-related meaning, you already have one strike against your success with the document project.

To be useful the statement must be a commonsense balance between detailed and general statements. It must be attractively laid out and simply written. No pomposities. No overcrowded copy. The test of a good statement lies in its usefulness. Test it. Ask the using people: "Is it useful?"

As the cop in the old TV series (Dragnet) used to say, "Just give me the facts, ma'am. Just the facts." No dreams. No "should be doings." No hoped-for responsibilities.

9. SET ASIDE ALL COMMON DUTIES

There are certain types of work that are common duties of all departments. They are not specifically assigned, but every group has them. Such work is a part of the "housekeeping" functions of every department and every section. There is no value (to the reader) of listing these common duties on each statement of work. Confine the work statements to the unique work of each group.

Identify work that is common to all groups. List such activities, then issue them as a separate document. Do not include common duties in a statement of work.

Develop and distribute one statement covering these common duties. Then strip them out of any department's statements. Head up the statement with the title: COMMON DUTIES. Typical of common duties are these examples:

1. Secure departmental supplies and materials.
2. Store and issue supplies for department use.
3. Prepare yearly budgets and forecasts.
4. Initiate the hiring and firing of employees*
5. Train (or provide for the training of) new employees.
6. Schedule vacation for employees.
7. Coordinate with departments doing related work.
8. Make periodical reports to superiors.
9. Distribute pay checks.
10. Approve requisitions.
11. Dictate and issue memos.
12. Attend meetings.
13. Transfer an employee.
14. Evaluate an employee.
15. Request office layout changes.
16. Prepare a request for expenditure for a capital item.
17. Set up and maintain files.
18. Request services from data processing.
19. Arrange for a change of telephone service.

Of course, you'll discover unique common duties for your company. Add them to the list.

Do not burden your reader with departmental statements that are padded with common duties. Refer to such as "normal housekeeping" duties. Every department, every section, and every division has them.

10. STEPS IN WRITING A STATEMENT

1. Repeat the CHART TITLE. It must be the same as the department name. EXAMPLES:

*If the department is PERSONNEL, then statement 4 (on hiring and firing employees) would reflect a specialized type of work. It should be included and expanded upon in the Personnel Department's statements.

TRANSPORTATION or EMPLOYMENT or FABRICATION or PURCHASING or INTERNAL AUDITING. Write that title at the top of the statement, like this:

Statement of Work

on

MANUFACTURING CONTROL

2. SUMMARY. Summarize the department's total work in one or two sentences. Here's an example of such a summary for MANUFACTURING CONTROL, using two sentences:

    a. Plans and schedules all production work and releases work lots to the factory.
    b. Reports to management on the status of all work in process in production, tooling, materiel, and engineering.

3. EXPANDED STATEMENTS. Next expand that summary*. Explain each major subduty or "work package." Each block on the department's organization chart requires one or more work sentences. Write simple, direct sentences.

4. NOT OVER 20 EXPANDED STATEMENTS. If the total quantity of expanded statements exceeds 20, re-examine them. Strike out any common duties. Summarize minor work elements. Do not exceed two single-spaced typewritten pages (two sides of one sheet of paper).

5. LAYOUT. The typewritten line must not exceed 5½″ in width. Use pica spacing, which provides 10 characters (or spaces) to the inch. Use a ro-

---

*Some writers prefer to write the series of expanded statements first and then go back and create the work summary.

man, not a sans-serif, type face. Leave generous white space margins at the top, bottom, and sides of the paper. One inch of such border space is a minimum.

6. USE APPROVED WORK WORDS. Start each statement with a strong verb. Consult your company's list of "work words." (We will provide a starter word list a little further on in this chapter.) Will one of those work words serve to describe a portion of the department's work? If you use another verb, *define* it.

7. CURRENT ACTIVITIES ONLY. Each statement reflects only what the department or section is doing *now*. Do not state what someone thinks the department should be doing . . . or what it plans to do even if that duty has been assigned. It must be work currently performed, must have active people and a financial budget.

8. AVOID COMMON DUTIES. Do not state common duties. EXAMPLES: Hiring people, transferring people, planning*, firing, conferring, or writing memos. Every department does those things. Every department orders supplies, requests a desk, asks for a change in telephone service, or asks for data processing services. Do not state common activities.

9. SUMMARIZE MINOR SUPPORT SERVICES. Summarize minor duties in one sentence. EXAMPLE: If one person operates a "blueprint" machine, turning out prints of engineering drawings, do not make a separate statement. Summarize such a minor support service as "provides prints."

---

*A duty that is common, in most units, can become the major reason for another group's existence. EXAMPLE: The four people now comprising your long-range planning office should state their various planning activities. Planning is *their* work specialty. To all others, planning is a common duty.

10. AVOID TASK OUTLINES. Make the statement of
     work about a *group* of people, not about an indi-
     vidual's tasks. If one person's work IS vital to
     the department's activity, state it. EXAMPLE: One
     research engineer's work in the way-out-state-
     of-the-art field of engineering magnetics, a de-
     velopment that may put the company "out in
     front."

11. NO JOB DESCRIPTIONS. Statements of work describe
     only the work or the responsibilities of a *group* of
     people. (By contrast, a job description describes
     one person's position or job.) Groups may be de-
     partments, sections, gangs, units, or divisions.

12. NOT WHAT THE BOSS DOES. Do not write what the
     manager or supervisor does. Write what his or
     her group does. If, in a small group, the super-
     visor does some of the work, treat his work as
     part of the group's effort.

11. USE WORK WORDS

Since we are making statements about work, the action words
themselves should be carefully selected "work words" . . . active
verbs in their simplest form and carefully defined.

The following work words and their definitions can serve as
starters for your list of functional verbs. Of course each organization does work that is unique to it and additions to this list will
be necessary.

If any other work words are used on a statement of work,
secure definitions from the person who uses them.

Only by limiting the verbs used can the top executives cross-
examine or cross-check several activities that seem to be the
same. If 15 different work groups say they *control,* do they control the same things? If six different work groups say they *administer* . . . how does this administrative activity uniquely fit in?
Here's a starter list of work words:

Words For Use on Management Documents

Work Words	Definitions
Accomplishes	Gets a result of value to the organization. Brings either routine or project work to a successful completion.
Accumulates	Brings together, collects, amasses.
Administers	Directs others in the execution of work. Here the department itself doesn't *do* the work. Accepts progress reports and takes corrective action.
Analyzes	Studies a problem to discover causes and symptoms. Finds relationships and prepares to offer alternative solutions. Takes apart. Examines components.
Assigns	Allots a job. Gives someone a piece of work to do.
Approves	Officially sanctions. Gives a "go ahead." O.K.'s. Has the authority to approve.
Conducts	Leads, guides, directs, or escorts. Supervises, but *does not do* the work.
Controls	Exercises the power to stop, start, make, move, or to change what other people do.
Coordinates	Brings many ideas, or efforts, or views into a single plan for action or an agreement. Secures a compromise or satisfactory solution to differences between people or groups of people.
Creates	Brings into reality or originates something of value that didn't exist before. Includes combining old, existing values into a unique new value.
Develops	Causes to grow. Guides toward fulfillment.
Edits	Revises and prepares for publication. Inspects for accuracy or for acceptable quality. Reads proof. Rejects substandard results. Calls for rewrites.
Establishes	Starts something new, gets a new activity into full operation. Launches an activity and pushes it until it is on "firm ground."

Words For Use on Management Documents *(continued)*

Work Words	*Definitions*
Evaluates	Based on facts gathered, weighs and interprets those facts. Measures. Compares what should be to what is.
Forecasts	From a study of past results and other factual criteria, such as trends, predicts future changed circumstances.
Formulates	Reduces to a written, useful product or statement. Puts together.
Furthers	Promotes, helps a program to move forward or toward a goal. Develops.
Implements	Gives practical effect to a plan or concept. Applies it. Starts it. Puts a plan, such as a new system, to work and to use.
Initiates	Same as "establishes," but may not go beyond "starting."
Installs	Establishes in place. Sets up. Puts into operation.
Issues	Passes out, delivers, gives out, mails, sends, distributes.
Maintains	Supports. Keeps from declining. Updates. Gradually improves. Prevents or repairs breakdowns.
Measures	Finds the extent, quantity, degree, size, quality, or capacity (by reference to a standard).
Operates	Works. Performs day-to-day work that gets results. Carries on an assigned routine mission, task, or project.
Performs	Executes. Does work. Carries on work that gets results (similar in meaning to "operation").
Plans	Schemes. Selects a path to follow to a goal. Prepares for action. Outlines a course of action. Makes and coordinates arrangements.

Words For Use on Management Documents *(continued)*

Work Words	*Definitions*
Prepares	Makes ready.
Processes	Alters. Changes. Adds. Works on.
Produces	Fabricates. Assembles. Brings forth. Makes. Manufactures.
Provides	Supplies. Gives something needed to an individual or to a group of individuals.
Recommends	Suggests, often as a staff duty. Consults. Advises. Urges.
Reviews	Examines critically. Judges. Concludes.
Schedules	Develops a plan based on a series of steps completed within specific time spans.
Secures	Makes fast. Obtains possession óf. Keeps safely. Prevents loss.
Submits	Offers as an opinion. Recommends. Surrenders. Yields. Suggests.

Since the department heads (or their staffers) will originate the drafts on their statements of work, they will need various guides, including:

1. The 12 writing guides
2. Your list of acceptable work words
3. What work to include, and to exclude
4. Several examples of completed statements

Since the manager will originate the draft statements, provide him or her with writing guides and other aids.

Give the department writer some personal guidance also. Show him or her how to put the foregoing aids to use. The last guide is "What Work to Include?"

12. WHAT WORK TO INCLUDE?

What work should be stated? What work should not be stated? Consider these suggestions:

1. **Hours Consumed by the Work.** How many total manhours does the department consume in a week? Does the work you are about to state use a large percentage of the department's total employee hours? Would it be 3 percent, 7 percent, or 10 percent?

   EXAMPLE: If the department has 100 people with each employee working a standard work week of 36 hours, that department uses 3,600 manhours per week. If one of the jobs requires an expenditure of 900 manhours (one quarter of the total) it is certainly important enough to describe. If another job consumes only 30 hours in a week (less than 1 percent of the department's total) it is doubtful whether it should be written separately. It can be summarized along with other minor duties.

2. **Work That is Unique or Different.** Is the work that you are describing *distinctly* different from work that people do in some other department? It must have at least one person who has the responsibility for doing that work. EXAMPLE: In a transportation department, the basic duty is to operate trucks. However, the department also provides a messenger service using three station wagons. Drivers carry documents from building to building. So that is a distinct, different duty. It IS a form of transportation, but it is different from operating trucks. So state it briefly: "Provides inter-building messenger service."

3. **Include a Statement on the "Big Show."** Every department or unit of the organization has its own "big show," the basic work reason for that unit's existence. State that work prominently.

4. **Relative Importance of the Work.** How important (to the entire organization) is the work you are about to describe? The work may not con-

sume many hours but it may be a highly important job. Its importance may be out of proportion to the time it consumes. Even a 20-hour-a-week job could be a key duty.

5. **A Separate Organization Box.** Is a work term shown in a separate box on the department's official organization chart? If so, write at least one sentence that describes that work.

REMINDER. On the department's statement drafts, ask the writer (department head or supervisor) to indicate the staff size required to execute the work reflected by each sentence. Also get the yearly budget figures. EXAMPLE:

```
Constructs and maintains standard, special or

perishable tooling in accordance with tool

design drawings, specifications and tooling orders
```
BUDGET $210K (12)

Top executives will be interested in staff size in relation to a work statement. Remove these figures before publishing and distributing the copies. Later you could add these figures to individual copies for key executives.

13. THE CHIEF EXECUTIVE'S ANNOUNCEMENT

To insure that your documents program will succeed, the chief executive officer must believe in its value and really want it. Do not attempt such a program without top-level approval.

The chief first announces the program at one of his staff meetings. He tells his subordinate vice-presidents what the program will consist of and its value to all. He tells them that *they* will originate the drafts but will have guidance from you. You will serve both as editor and as document coordinator.

Every man and woman whose name is shown either on the basic organization chart or on the six or eight major department charts, needs to be aware of the program. Send out an announcement over the chief executive officer's signature. It could read something like this:

To: All department heads, managers, and supervisors
From: The President
Subject: Statements of Work

Starting on 1 March 19XX we will begin the development of a series of management documents entitled "Statements of Work." These will be write-ups reflecting each work activity of every department. In effect, the initial phase of the program will result in taking a complete work inventory.

We want to know who does what work now and in what department. This information could be an eye opener for all of us. I will take a personal interest in each document.

The responsibility for originating the department's statement of work falls on the department head. However, guidance will be available on what to write and how to write it. The guidance must be used. We must avoid torrents of fancy words and euphemisms that would be of no value. We want only facts regarding current work and such facts stated in plain English.

Do not write up activities assigned but not performed, nor activities hoped for or planned. Write up only the work that your people are performing TODAY. Each "package of work" will be reflected in a simple, short sentence. At the end of each sentence (on the right margin), indicate the total number of employees now required to execute the work. Also show the yearly budget required, including salaries. The total staff for each work sentence must add up to the total staff count of the department, minus the department head. The added staff and budget notations will not be published in the finalized documents.

Over a period of several months we will publish one statement for each department. These will be distributed to all management manual holders.

Subsidiary statements may be developed within departments but these will not be maintained by our management documents officer. Department statements will

be reviewed, updated, and if necessary, reissued quarterly.
Reasonable deadlines for the drafts, revisions, and final drafts will be set and adhered to. The plan is to issue one department's statement of work at a time.

ROBERT M. MCMILLAN, *President*

14. PRINCIPLES OF MANAGEMENT

Principles of effective management do impinge on the structure of an organization. So let's consider such principles as they were written in the French language and translated into English in the mid-1920s.

Second only to Frederick W. Taylor in stature of the scientific management movement (1895 to 1935) is Henri Fayol, a French manager whose teaching as well as whose practice revolved around the *management* functions. Monsieur Fayol was a practical leader/manager. He guided a huge but nearly bankrupt mining and industrial works organization to immense success and prosperity in the early 1900s. (By contrast, Mr. Taylor concentrated on the facets of how *individuals* could be more productive.) Monsieur Fayol summarized five functions of management as:

1. Planning
2. Organizing
3. Commanding
4. Controlling
5. Coordinating

Obviously, if any manager tries to work in ignorance of the work now being performed, he could not do those five things well. Many chief executives today do not know what work all their people are doing. So they find it hard to decide how their companies should be organized.

It is in Fayol's function 2, organizing, where the statement of work is an essential tool. Function 3, commanding, can be largely handled through the various management systems since 90 percent of the organization's daily work is done through its network of systems.

In addition to the five essential functions, Fayol also offered 14 principles of management which he said he needed to apply most frequently. Briefly, they are:

1. Division of work into specialties	8. Centralization
2. Authority required	9. Line of authority (scalar chain of command)
3. Discipline	
4. Unity of command	10. Order
5. Unity of direction	11. Equity
6. Subordination of individual interest	12. Stability of employee tenure
7. Remuneration	13. Initiative
	14. Esprit de corps

By *dividing the work,* the higher productivity of specialization is possible. When men and women work as specialists, the total output goes up.

Authority is the right to give orders and the power to exact obedience. The *discipline** of any group of men or women depends essentially upon the worthiness of that group's leader. The best worker doesn't always make the best supervisor. Yet in appointing new supervisors, managers make this mistake millions of times. They promote the wrong people and leave them to operate at their level of incompetence.

Unity of command means that each person takes orders only from one superior. In this respect, Fayol pointed out that duties are often badly defined. This creates an ever present danger of dual command. Such dual command is a perpetual source of conflict and a lowering of productivity.

Fayol defines *unity of direction* as "one head and one plan for the group of people having the same objective." The individual's interest must be subordinated to the general interest. There must be absolutely no conflict of interest.

Remuneration is simply the pay that employees receive for their services. It also includes bonuses and any shares of profit. Today it includes the fringe benefits so widely provided.

There must be *centralization* of direction and control. Fayol

*For enlightenment on this essential management subject read the clearly written book *Discipline or Disaster,* Magoon & Richards, 1966, Exposition Press, New York.

says, "This principle turns on the fact that in every organism, animal or social, sensations converge toward the brain or the directive part . . . and it is from the brain that orders are sent out which set all parts of the organism in a *coordinated movement!*"

The *line of authority*, the scalar chain or chain of command, is the linkage of subordinates to superiors, ranging from the top or ultimate authority to the lowest ranks. This is the hierarchy. Fayol felt that people at the supervisory level, for example, should not always have to go up the chain of command through their immediate superiors to get some question resolved (perhaps by the president), but that supervisors must work out any problem between them, and only then inform their superiors. (Policy can be useful here.) Think of how often this principle is violated today, particularly in government. No wonder it takes six months to get a decision that takes less than 20 minutes to make. A judicious use of policy can vastly increase the lateral action capabilities of supervisors.

Fayol's principle of *order* is that "there is a place for everything and everything must be in its place." For people it is a "place for everyone and everyone performing in his or her place."

Equity is a combination of communication and justice.

Tenure of personnel is important since time is required for any employee to get used to new work and to be able to do it well. This principle requires reasonable stability. High employee turnover is very costly.

Initiative is the freedom (and official encouragement) to propose, and sometimes even to execute a project on the part of any *employee*. Here the guidance that we advocate, in the form of management documents, can permit a high degree of operational initiative.

Fayol said that animosity between departments or groups of people should be discouraged. Have them talk to each other face to face, not work by all written communications. This develops high-spirited* cooperation *(esprit de corps)*. The sensitive and skilled manager will coordinate effort, encourage individual keenness, and make full use of each man or woman's abilities. He will reward each one's merit without arousing jealousy or disturbing harmonious relations among the worker's peers.

---

*For management effectiveness in a "nutshell," read *Management Plus* Richard LeTourneau, 1973, Zondervan Books, Grand Rapids, MI.

Chapter 4

POLICY

Is It the Most Neglected Management Tool?

Policy is a major device that people could use to carry on the process of management. Yet how many people know what a policy really is? How many know how to use it? Policy, communicated and used well, is a powerful management tool . . . truly a document to manage by.

1. POLICY AS A VAGUE "SOMETHING"

My experience, in both large and small organizations, indicates that relatively few management people have a firm mental grasp of what policy is. Even some presidents and chief executives miss the point. In one organization the newly installed president (who did understand policy) invited me to attend one of his staff meetings. For my benefit he asked the 14 executives present:

What is policy? What words come to your mind?

Here are some of those senior officials' responses:

Rules . . . insurance . . . numbers racket
. . . company laws . . . excuses . . . goals . . .
procedures . . . instructions . . . regulations . . . laws . . . a way of management
. . . arbitrary decisions . . . objectives . . .
authority . . . planning . . . strait jackets
. . . what the boss wants . . . an excuse for
not doing something.

79

Those men and women were corporate officers. Some ran large departments. The company had no policy manual and issued no documents entitled POLICY. It was clear that not one "top-drawer" executive really understood policy. So naturally they had not been using policy as a management tool.

Later, in another organization, I conducted a seminar on "Systems for Executives." During the session I asked the group of 25 administrators and executives to tell what they thought policy was. Some gave two or three opinions. It was clear that here, too, policy was a vague something. The responses fell roughly into these categories:

	No. of Ideas
It is a statement	28
A decision by top management	13
Rules	14
A guide	9
The president's desires	7
A series of no-no's	4

Other words came from those people in response to the question, "What is a *synonym* for policy?" The ideas expressed were:

> Regulation . . . company laws . . . plans . . . moral principles . . . instructions . . . company's position . . . government . . . objectives.

In my earlier work as a senior systems analyst I also felt that policy seemed to be a vague something. People used the term frequently but it was evident that few people understood it. And I was among them. Oddly enough policy seemed so often to be a stumbling block to a good system that I just had to dig into the subject.

2. THE NON-USE OF POLICY

In discussing policy with the corporate manager of systems in one of our larger organizations, he said that he had to search hundreds of memos in order to find what policies undergirded the systems that his analysts were working on. His company did not provide a policy document. Neither was there, anywhere, a definition of what policy was.

Another organization did have a document entitled POLICY, but the people used it for many purposes. It was most often used to announce staff changes . . . or promotions . . . transfers of management and staff men and women . . . all nonpolicy matters. It was clear that again these people didn't know what policy was. EXAMPLE: A staff change has nothing to do with policy. It is an organization structure change, a shift of individuals.

Some management men and women do understand policy (often in smaller companies) but they do not wish to state it. They know that it restricts them as well as anyone else in the organization. The president of a smaller company said:

> I do not intend to write my various policies. If I did, I would be bound by them. I'd rather remain free to make my decisions on these matters as they come up.

I know from my own observation (as a documents consultant) that that president lost some of his hours each day because he took the time to answer questions that his operating people could have answered just as well . . . if they had policy guidance.

If an executive will not accept the discipline of his own policies, it is difficult for the operating people to make good decisions. Also it is almost impossible for that executive to delegate effectively. He would give a NO answer on a subject one day and a YES answer the next day, confusing his employees.

Other executives said they would rather issue policy on interoffice memos. The reason: "To reduce paperwork." One vice-president said she didn't want to state policy in her large department because "it destroys initiative on the part of my operating people." Her experience may have been that someone wrote "policy" by going into a tremendous amount of detail, telling people "when to pick up or lay down a pencil."

Even when the organization does have a document entitled POLICY, the managers use it for many purposes. These can range from statements of work for a specific department, to staff changes, to plain announcements, to procedures, to work instructions, or as reminders. Any of those documents could be useful, yet none of them are policy.

A worker in the operations area needs specific guidance so he can make good decisions.

Part of the weakness in policy use is the inability of the policy
writer to make the statement clear.

Many policies are too detailed. If a "policy" is written in detail
and it requires somebody to follow it letter by letter, is it really
policy? The bureaucratic idea of going "strictly by the book" is
the result of policies that are too detailed. If you put out a policy
statement that is too detailed, you will indeed lose the value of
common sense that your operating people could apply to a local
situation. But a policy statement can be too general. Consider
this excerpt:

> It is the firm and continuing policy of this company to
> operate effectively and economically in all aspects of its
> operations in order to serve its customers, employees,
> stockholders and the communities in which it operates.

One man read that policy excerpt and pronounced it "hogwash." It is so general that it would be hard to see how such a statement could guide any employee. On the other hand, a statement someone meant to be a policy could be too detailed, such as:

> Prefix or suffix numbers shall no longer be added to our previously issued part or assembly numbers. Henceforth the policy provides there is to be assigned only one part number for any one part, detail, sub-assembly, or final assembly, so no dual or additional identification of any components will be permitted. The final assembly number will serve as a synonym for the model number and both the assembly and the part number will be used as catalog numbers. Assignment of a model number immediately precludes the use of an entire series of part numbers.

3. WHAT IS A POLICY?

How do we identify policy? How do we develop it? How do we use it? Maintain it? What role does top or middle management play in that development? Do the operating people play any role at all in policy development? Specifically who has the ability to write a useful policy?

If an organization does not issue any policy statements, what advantages could it be losing? If a company issues too many policies, what happens? What is the result if policies are not well-written? Or if all policies are unwritten? Or not correctly distributed? Do people really *use* policy? Can anyone make an exception to a specific policy?

Before we consider those questions, look at an example of a useful policy statement. It did the work for the purpose for which it was designed:

> 1. All full time employees, when first hired, will serve a three (3) month probationary period. This period is for the benefit of both the Company and the individual employee.

2. An employee does not have the status of a permanent, regular employee until his or her probationary period has been satisfactorily completed.

3. After satisfactorily completing such probationary period, an employee will then be considered permanent and will then be eligible to receive the current employee benefits including those relating to medical, sick leave, vacations, insurance, and other benefits that are now or will be available to all employees.

That policy, of course, relates to Personnel (human resource) matters. But it also illustrates one important aspect of policy . . . which is to provide for the "fair and uniform treatment of all people."

So that's the usual situation. Most managers don't really understand policy, so, of course, they don't use it as a management tool. How about supervisors . . . those members of management who are on the "firing line"? Do they do any better? We had 33 supervisors in a briefing session on management documentation and asked: "What is policy?" Their answers can be summarized as:

1. Policy is the same as a procedure.

2. It is like a procedure, only at a higher level.

3. It's authority and responsibility.

4. Policy is an excuse for what we do.

5. It is what the board of directors decides on.

6. Policy is what my boss wants.

7. It is the goal of the organization.

8. Policy covers the business ethics of our company.

9. Policy is such a vague thing that it is useless for us to even talk about it.

10. It is a group of high-sounding platitudes that have no application to our daily work.

But there has been some good thinking on the subject of policy, in an out of organizations. Consider these definitions of policy that have been offered by students of policy, particularly leading educators:

1. A policy is a statement of a course of action to be consistently followed under stated conditions without reference to higher authority. . . . *Dr. H. C. Grant, Toronto*

2. Policies are strong coordinative influences that can hold the organization together wherever the division of labor is used . . . and where departments that are not naturally cooperative in character but are included in the total enterprise. . . . *Kimball and Kimball*

3. Policy should be the framework of meaning to business plans in order that the decisions made will follow through this framework and will be consistent with such plans. Policies go beyond company objectives. Policies are meant to be guides for thinking, while procedures are guides to action. . . . *Dr. Harold Koontz*

4. A business organization is ultimately a device for doing things and for getting results. If it devotes too much of its effort and attention to the process of deciding what to do, it will fail to establish effective arrangements to do what has been decided. In such circumstances, without formal organization, the attention and ambition of key people who should be concentrating on the action phases will be devoting their time and energies to debating policies. Individuals in the organization who should be devoting themselves to executing the action will give the lion's share of their efforts and time to influencing policy decisions or to obstructing those decisions if they disagree with them. . . . *Lyndall Urwick*

If policies are not written and distributed to
the men and women who can use them, they
must resort to the torturous chain of command. The chain of command is necessary
because of the division of work into numerous specialties, but it is a notoriously poor
"channel of communication."

The result of the situation described by Mr. Urwick is to weaken the organization because deciding and then redeciding will consume the time that key people should be devoting to action and instead they will be debating, manipulating . . . or politicking.

Adequate policy guidance in an organization is not an optional luxury. It is not extra "paperwork." It is NECESSARY. If the executives do not provide policy guidance, they leave a vacuum in the management process. Other people, including the operators, will move into the vacuum and try to fill it. Then the top executives will wonder why their plans are not being well executed at the working level.

The following definitions are my own. They all came out of experience and they have proven to be useful:

1. Policy is a *decision*. It helps all employees involved in the area that the decision covers to follow an approved course of action. Managers "make" a policy after weighing alternatives. Such a decision can be applied to any number of similar transactions in the future by other people.

2. Policy provides a *single direction* in which all people in the organization can go. Usually a policy must be translated into an action plan that can be explained by a related procedure and backed up by a key printed form.

3. Policy is a statement that explains the correct *course of action* that people are to follow when they encounter an identifiable problem. They can then act without seeking a decision from a higher authority.

In addition to those three definitions, this four-point summary has been helpful:

1. Policy is *what* management wants.

2. Policy is a consistent way of *treating all people.* "People," in this definition, includes employees,

customers, stockholders, vendors, and the general community.

3. Policy is a single decision that can be applied to all similar questions or problems in the future.

4. Policy points to a single direction in which all organized activity is to flow.

Oddly enough all policy definitions haven't been as useful as have the following twelve *characteristics* of policy. Let's say you have a document in front of you. What is it? Procedure? Policy? You can use these characteristics to identify that document (or the parts of it) that are policy. Here are the characteristics:

1. It does not tell people how to *proceed*.

2. It reflects a *decision* that can be used rather widely.

3. It is *what* management wants.

4. It helps supervisors and operating people to make sound decisions on the *operating level*.

5. It provides for *fair treatment* of all people. (This is extremely important.)

6. It brings *consistency* into numerous operations.

7. It provides a *unity of purpose*. It points all segments of the organization in a single, goal-seeking direction.

8. It tends to point to the definite objective of the organization . . . to its goals.

9. It *relieves top executives* from the job of making routine decisions repeatedly.

10. It can be applied in most similar situations.

11. With policy, good decisions can be made at the operating level.

12. It answers the *what* to do part of a question.

Let's see how those characteristics apply. Here is a policy statement relating to blood bank donations:

> It is the Company's policy and the desire of management to cooperate fully with the Red Cross and its blood bank program. Arrangements have been made for mobile facilities to visit the plant for two days every three months. The visits will be announced in the monthly newsletter. The time required for blood donations (about one hour) will be considered time worked for wage purposes. Instructions for charging the time can be obtained from any timekeeper. Personnel will schedule the donations.

Notice this about that short policy, based on the characteristics just listed:

1. It does not tell how to *proceed*.
2. Reflects a *decision* that applies widely.
3. Is what management *wants*.
4. Helps operating people to make sound decisions.
5. Treats all people fairly.
6. Brings consistency to operations.
7. It is in harmony with the company's goals (such as being a good neighbor).
8. Relieves top executives from making repeated decisions.
9. Can be applied to similar situations.
10. Supervisors can make decision at the operating level.
11. It answers the *what* to do part of a question.
12. Can be applied repeatedly in the future.

Of course most policy statements will not have all 12 characteristics. But if a document has seven or eight of the characteristics it probably is a statement of policy.

4. LOSSES WITHOUT POLICY

One thing that operating people look for in their managers is reasonable consistency. If the executives understand policy and use it correctly, the men and women who use policy will soon "catch on." They'll begin to understand and to apply policy profitably.

However, if management's documents are inconsistent, nonexistent, poorly written, or unwisely distributed, then their usefulness is questionable. Better to continue to put all management communication on memos and let communication confusion reign.

The losses that an organization suffers from a lack of well-used policies are mostly intangible and largely unprovable in dollars. So we must resort to common sense and ask questions such as these:

1. If operating people have adequate guidance, can't *they* make good decisions?

2. If policy guides are distributed well, will the executives have *more time* for other matters?

3. Can *delegation* be more complete if the delegatee has written guidance?

4. What, other than policies, can help management to "steer" the company's activities toward its goals?

5. If there is inadequate policy guidance isn't it likely that:

    a. The request for many important decisions must move slowly up the "chain of command"?

    b. Or that people at the operating level are likely to make decisions that are not consistent and do not point goalward?

Here are other problems that exist because policy is lacking. If the action at the bottom of the hierarchy in the organization is too slow, the company becomes a hog-tied giant. If, on the other

Policy statements can help point all effort toward the organization's goals.

hand, it is fast but not correct, then operating people could be pulling in the wrong direction. Documentation can be inconsistent. And when it is, any attempts at communication are ineffective. In one company the executive vice-president used a policy bulletin to announce the creation of a committee. In this bulletin he named the members of the committee and spelled out their various responsibilities. *That is not policy at all!* Anyone who has analyzed organizations knows that announcing an organization's new setup and its responsibility is a *statement of work*. It doesn't make any difference whether the activity is assigned to a permanent group such as a department or a section . . . or to a temporary body such as a committee.

Lack of policy can result in rigor mortis in the action arenas. Requests for decisions must move, like molasses in January, up the torturous chain of command. Or the decision will be made only after people hold a long series of meetings.

When operating people lack policy guidance, they tend to develop their own guidance. It may or may not be the kind of guidance that the top managers would approve.

There are two diverse types of interest in any organization . . . the *corporate* interest (general interest) versus the *individual* interest of each employee. But by its very nature, the welfare of the organization must transcend any individual's personal welfare. Otherwise the organization cannot continue to exist and both corporate and personal interests will evaporate.

There are no vacuums in policy. One man, at a high level in a medium-sized organization, maintained that it is not necessary to state and then to communicate policy to the employees. He said: "Such documents create too much paper work. We'll have none of it."

What he didn't recognize was that if he doesn't fill the need for policy, someone else will. The man or woman at the working level must take action; they must carry on the work that has been assigned to them.

Supervisors often develop policy and then "distribute" it orally, usually by telling an employee what he did wrong.

Any management tool must be handy . . . or it won't be used. If true policies are scattered through memos and letters and miscellaneous documents, those policy statements are not useful. And, of course, people who don't recognize policy for what it is, and the fact that they are stating it in a memo, will go on doing so. One student of management said:

> Policy formulation is a legislative process even when you find it in the executive branch or in the judiciary. It is legislative because it establishes laws or rules that are to be followed by those who execute those laws.

It is a sad waste when any executive must hunt through filed reports, memos, letters, and miscellaneous documents in order to find a policy that will apply to a problem that she faces at the moment. A new employee in the organization must fumble and probe in order to find out what the policies are that impinge upon his or her work. This lack does not make for speedy, decisive, or flexible actions.

Because policies that are buried in memos are not coordinated, one statement can directly contradict another statement of policy. So people at the action level receive confusing directions.

5. VALUES FROM POLICY

The effective corporation is one that possesses an invisible asset . . . unusually *good internal teamwork*. And policy can aid substantially in developing such teamwork. With adequate policy guidance, each man and each woman, operator or president, can use the same action signals. Consistent signals tend to weave individual efforts into a single, corporate direction. The concept is this:

> Each action, each decision, each effort in the organization harmonizes with every other action, decision, or effort. And that means corporate POWER!

Policy provides a common point of reference for all people. If one supervisor makes a decision at one time, what she decided will be consistent with a decision that another supervisor will make a few months later . . . even though in a different work area.

EXAMPLE: A senior engineer received a brochure on a conference on the state of the art in his engineering specialty. He wondered whether the company would favor his attendance and pay the costs (travel, etc.). He felt that to serve his company as well as to further his own career, he should be on the "cutting edge" of research and development in his specialty. So he asked his supervisor if she would approve the trip. The supervisor, without policy guidance, went to the assistant chief engineer (the chief was out of town), who turned down the request.

A policy tends to treat all people in the organization fairly.

A few months later another engineer, in a different department, took a similar request to his supervisor, who took the question to the chief engineer, who approved the trip. And inevitably the first engineer (and his supervisor) heard about it. A year later a job opening occurred in a competitive firm and the first engineer took that job, leaving a vital project without a project manager. The turn-down wasn't the only reason, but to that man the company's decision to let one person go to a conference and not another was inconsistent and he looked upon such actions as a sign of poor management.

A summary of the advantages of using a policy includes some of the following:

1. Use of policy tends to prevent deviation from planned courses of action that would lead to the organization's goals.

2. Policy increases the assurance that the organization will enjoy consistency in its management decisions.

3. Policy can promote intelligent cooperation between and among people.

4. A well-stated policy permits the intelligent exercise of initiative at the operating level.

5. Policy can become the basis for determining the quality of any executive action.

6. Policy can provide a guide for people whose job it is to plan for the future.

7. A well-stated policy can supply the organization with a code of law for its internal "government," with positives and negatives.

8. Policy can reduce the requirement for top dictatorial leadership.

9. A clear policy statement provides a standard to which all people in the organization can adhere.

10. By *writing* one policy and by having access to all other written and issued policies, there is less possibility of one policy contradicting the other.

If you are working toward a goal, consistency of your actions will be an asset. Inconsistency causes fumbling and confusion. Grasshopper actions do not lead to a goal.

With well-considered and clearly stated policies the turmoil from a parade of "new brooms" will be minimized. Policy brings consistency, continuity, and stability . . . all *corporate* virtues.

Constant, unnecessary change is absolutely *inconsistent* with the corporate concept, which is an entity that lives on, even though its individual members may die.

Consider delegation. Won't an organization do well if every possible action decision can be made by an operator yet be consistent with the corporate goals?

Talk about "job enrichment." If the receiving clerk on the dock can make good decisions all day without running to his supervisor, isn't he going to feel "pretty good" about his job?

When you study policy, it becomes clear that the policy decision itself is a "master decision." And numerous subdecisions can be derived from it. The corporation gains strength because operating decisions are being made at the operating level, yet they are consistent with the short-and long-term company goals.

Personnel people are probably the leading users of policy. They seem to understand it best. However, the need for policy goes beyond personnel matters. Most areas of activity require policy guidance. Some of this guidance is limited to a specific type of work such as *purchasing policies* . . . or *sales policies*. Other policies apply universally to all segments of the organization. The following list gives an idea of the range of needed policies:

1.	How to use consultants	13.	Auditing
2.	Per diem payments	14.	Professional societies
3.	Advertising	15.	Bank accounts
4.	Sales	16.	Contributions
5.	Insurance	17.	Systems and computing
6.	Inventory pricing	18.	Data security
7.	Capital expenditures	19.	Training and development
8.	Public relations	20.	Company real estate
9.	News releases	21.	Company records
10.	Operating reports	22.	Use of company stationery
11.	Budgets		
12.	Quality standards		

23. Business cards	27. Travel expenses
24. Authority patterns	28. Plant and office
25. Purchasing	security
26. Employment and	29. Vacations
termination	30. Grievances

You've noticed the term FOB on invoices. Do you know what it means? It represents a policy decision. FOB means that the executives of the company decided to price an item as *Freight On Board* at their factory.

So you would pay the freight in addition to the cost of the item. Another policy decision could be FOB destination. Then the price you pay for the article will land it in your city.

One of the scarcest resources in any organization is the time of its officers, managers, and supervisors. Do not waste it. Once two or more executives have spent precious time to arrive at a policy decision, the organization then possesses an asset that didn't exist before. Quality policy, then, is an investment that can pay dividends for years to come. And the term "quality" must be equated with usefulness. So a quality policy achieves two gains:

1. It conserves executive time, time that can be used to solve other pressing executive-type problems.

2. It enables men and women in the operations arena to move *quickly* and *correctly*.

With policy guidance supervisors and their subordinate workers don't have to fumble and bumble around. Middle managers are not required to correct operating decisions.

One of the criticisms that you'll hear about reducing decisions to written policy is that it "stifles the initiative of the individual." Of course we want initiative at all levels, but not the freedom for people to go spinning off onto tangents. We must have *teamwork*. The organization itself is a device for making teamwork possible.

A clearly stated policy provides a single point of reference for all people in the organization.

Hence there can never be absolute freedom for each employee to do what he or she wants to do. To a reasonable extent each individual's freedom in the work place must be subordinated to the objectives of the entire corporation . . . for the "good of the ship."

Is initiative desirable? Yes, you bet. We all want it. But we must also have unity of direction. Policy guidance can be used to permit the utmost personal initiative consistent with the organization's teamwork requirements.

6. DEVELOPING POLICY

Policy is a master decision. After executives make that decision, someone must write that decision so clearly that it can guide operating people in making *derived* decisions.

Before arriving at a basic (policy) decision, somebody must investigate the situation. Who will do this investigating, this fact gathering? The executive himself or herself? Or a staff assistant?

> ADVICE: Appoint one *capable* person as *the* staff officer to develop and maintain all management documents. This includes organization charts, statements of work, policies, "big show" procedures, and the official approval authority document.

What are the steps the documents officer will take to develop policy? Here is a rather "sure fire" sequence that the developer will follow in developing a policy statement:

1. First, there's the "trigger." A problem or a question arises repeatedly that requires executive or supervisory attention.

2. This problem comes to the attention of one or more executives or the policy developer discovers the need.

3. The developer studies the situation. He (or she) sets forth two or three alternative courses of action to be considered.

4. He recommends one of those alternatives.

5. He explains the probable effects of each of these alternatives. Note: The developer's alternative is not yet written as a useful policy. It is more complete than the final policy statement will be and is in the form of a "special report."

6. The executives make a final decision.

7. The developer then writes the decision in policy statement form and rechecks it with the executive or executives.

8. Coordination is next. The developer takes the approved statement to the department people who will use the policy. This coordination step helps to insure a quality (useful) policy.

9. Based on the user's advice, the developer revises, then finalizes the statement in reproducible form and secures the chief executive's signature.

10. Selects the correct distribution list and issues the policy statement.

11. Retains the back-up documentation that pertains to this policy, including the special report, other alternatives that were considered, the current conditions, the specific situation, and each executive's reasons for his or her final decision. The developer preserves this information in a work folder under the policy number.

Sooner or later someone will suggest a change in the policy, perhaps going back to the old one. In this folder the developer can find all the "reasons why" the old policy was abandoned and why other alternatives were not selected.

Now supervisors and operators can make snappy but *correct* decisions at the operations level. And "correct" means a decision that is in harmony with the corporate goal.

Provide some training on the use of policy. A few hours of orientation can make the program much more effective. Consider this: Many people do not know what policy is. Therefore they may not know how to use it. So an hour in "training" for supervisors and managers would be helpful. Give these people examples of the situation that calls for policy application and how to apply it. Also explain how rare exceptions can be made.

7. ANY EXCEPTION?

Should the policy provide for exceptions? Since a policy decision is usually a compromise, there are bound to be a few unusual circumstances that should be considered and an exception made. (However, a quality policy should be applied from 90 to 99 percent of the time.)

Policy exceptions can be an area fraught with danger. The first danger is making everything an exception. Then the original policy decision is smashed. Managers and supervisors must be hard-nosed about policy enforcement. They must never make exceptions lightly.

The second danger is that the operating people, observing that a series of exceptions have been made, interpret these as a *change* of the policy.

When you make an exception to a policy, be sure that people know that it was an exception and not a change in the policy.

You can't be too careful in making exceptions. If a higher executive makes an exception to policy, he may be reversing a subordinate supervisor's decision that was based squarely on the policy. This can be confusing. Is the policy no longer valid?

Any executive who makes one exception must explain to all that this *is* an exception, not a change of policy.

Check occasionally. Record the exceptions. Keep the information in the policy "case history" folder under the policy number. Ask: Does the basic policy need an overhaul?

There's still another danger in making policy exceptions. The danger lies in *who* is making the exception. Ordinarily only the executive who approved the policy makes the exceptions. Other people may make exceptions only if they are specifically delegated the authority to do so. The reason for such caution is obvious. If anybody can make exceptions, then the policy itself is dead.

8. POLICY'S RELATIVES

Policy is one of the documents to manage by. So, briefly, what is the relationship of policy to:

1. A statement of goals?
2. The organization chart?
3. Statements of work?
4. Procedures?
5. Authority to approve patterns?

Goal setting is one of the products of long-range planning. "Long range" means five years or longer. The goal factors include:

1. A written description of the goal or goals
2. Timing and scheduling
3. Quantities

Goal setting and long-range planning are big subjects, so we will not go into them in this book. However, the very basis of quality management documentation is the statement of goals.

Policy and its relatives, taken together, provide a set of powerful executive tools . . . documents to manage by.

Does the organization (represented by its top managers) know where it wants to go? Has it developed plans for going there? Answers to those questions are basic. Once the goal is known, the next steps line up something like this:

1. What kind of organization will be required? This includes the necessary people-skills.
2. What work must these people do?
3. What *policies* will help us move toward that goal?
4. What teamwork plans will we need? (What management systems and their related procedures?)

Because of the intangible nature of policy, it is easy for people to delve into things that aren't policy at all. The terms *policy, procedures, rules,* and *regulations* are often jumbled in people's thinking. Our own thinking was jumbled, too, until we finally set out to study and define policy. Management men and women use all manner of documents to communicate with employees, including:

1.	Policy statements	9.	Special reports
2.	Planning descriptions	10.	Directives
3.	Committee assignments	11.	Regulations and rules
4.	Budget plans	12.	Job instructions
5.	Organization charts	13.	Job descriptions
6.	Procedures	14.	Notices
7.	Staff promotions	15.	Announcements
8.	Statements of goals	16.	Approval authorities

Some people have resisted setting standards for the use of management documents. They say, "It's too much paperwork." But today's chaotic jungle of documents does add up to too much paperwork. Another evil is the combining panacea. Someone says, "Let's have one all-purpose document." And we can ask, "Why? What is gained? The total paper volume will be the same." Our long experience in this field of communication practically screams out this advice:

Use one specific document to serve one specific purpose!

Consider the relationship of policy to that vastly misunderstood document . . . the procedure. The term *procedure* is used in many ways. One person says, "I have a good procedure for handling incoming invoices." Strictly speaking that "procedure" is a method, but people could argue about the term *method*. Another worker says, "I just wrote a procedure to cover that." "Procedure" is often treated as a synonym for "system." In the minds of others *policy* and *procedure* are two names for the same thing.

In my quarter century of teaching *management* systems to over 10,000 people I had to define terms carefully. Otherwise any effective teaching would have been impossible.

So a procedure is a *written document.* It is not a method. It is not a system. The written document describes a system. In turn, a system is not a computer, but it often includes a computer. A system is a plan for teamwork. EXAMPLE: A purchasing system is a *plan* whereby buyers and supervisors and stockkeepers and clerks and receiving people can work on separate phases of the procurement function . . . yet they perform as a team.

The related purchasing procedure describes that teamwork plan. So the procedure is one part of the management system, just as the computer and its instructional programs are parts of the system.

Policies undergird any system. The systems plan must incorporate the applicable policies.

Policies are both negative and positive . . . shalls and shall nots. A policy is the *what* of the management decision. It will underlie the procedure, the *how* of that related system. Policies don't usually provide for implementation, for putting the decision to work. Procedures do.

The *organization chart* reveals the reporting and responsibility patterns. So policies that apply corporate-wide are approved by the chief executive officer, as shown on the chart. Other policies apply only within a single department. EXAMPLE: The vice-president of materiel may initiate, but may not finally approve, a policy relating to an employee's traveling expenses since many departments will be affected by such a policy. However, the

materiel chief does approve policies that affect his department
such as on "competitive bidding."

The *statement of work* is a close relative of the chart. It expands
the "work words" used on the chart and explains *exactly* what
work is included under the brief title on the chart. If the title on
the chart is FINANCE AND ACCOUNTING, the related statement of work explains in some detail what people in FINANCE
AND ACCOUNTING do. The man or woman in charge of FI-
NANCE AND ACCOUNTING has the right, and the obliga-
tion, to set policy to guide subordinates in that department.

The management tool that people usually refer to as the "authority to approve" document is related to policy more remotely.
This approval document does spell out who can approve what.
To some extent, it is another view of the statements of work. If a
supervisor in the PURCHASING department is responsible for
"petty cash purchases," she will probably also have the authority
to approve such purchases.

9. POLICY AND MANAGEMENT PRINCIPLES

In our organizations we hear about principles, regulations, and
rules. The government *regulates* trucking companies. A judge
hands down a *ruling*. A management consultant uses management *principles* to make a sick company well again.

Here we could get bogged down in semantics and argue for-
ever. So we won't do that. But let's consider a few management
devices as they relate to policy. A simple rule can enable supervisors to apply a policy. EXAMPLE:

POLICY: To reduce the danger of fire in the factory or
in the offices.

RULE: Absolutely no smoking (in the spray paint section).

Such terms as *private* or *no admittance* or *apply at the office* or
deliver in rear are all reflections of specific rules.

Henri Fayol, the great French industrialist, stressed the importance of the "single will" in the organization. Only a single
corporate will can develop "go" power.

This singleness of will is not usually the personal will of the chief executive officer, even though he does play a major role in its development. His vision of where the organization should go will be reflected in many policy decisions. But so will other people's ideas and visions.

Policy is a document that enables the chief executive officer to use the "bull horn" technique, going direct to all employees without violating the chain of command.

Managers will be interested in another concept . . . that of the "bull horn," a navy term. A typical chief executive must wonder sometimes if men and women at the operating levels are deliberately ignoring his or her wishes. The response seems to be weak at the desk or at the workbench. However, most people *do* want to support management. Yet orders traveling down the chain of command lose their "flavor" along the way. So people are not really clear on what the chief wants done.

Communication breaks down in the chain of command. Repeatedly it has proved to be a poor device for communication. For administration, the chain is fine. For communication, the chain is weak. Information simply does not reach the operating levels clearly.

So, policy offers an opportunity for a top executive to go directly to the people . . . to all the people with a clear message. Yet he does not violate the principle of "only one boss." A ship captain reaches all the ship's company through a bull horn. Civilian executives can do it with a series of clearly stated policies.

Systems improvements sometime result in a reduced need for employees. Here's a brief policy statement on the subject:

> Any employee who participates in systems improvement work in his or her area need not have any concern that he or she will in any way be the loser due to the improvements that will result.

Systems analysts need a policy of that type. Why? Because if just one employee is adversely affected by a systems improvement, the word about this "unfair" treatment will get around fast. If one employee feels that his or her job status, salary, or other job factors have suffered due to improvements, that individual will be reluctant to cooperate on any systems improvement activity in the future. Worse, other employees, who will hear about the downgrading or the dismissal, will not be inclined to take part or cooperate in future improvement efforts.

Such a policy must be approved by the chief executive officer and adhered to and enforced. Usually attrition solves the problem and the now not-needed employee can be assigned to a comparable job elsewhere.

It isn't enough just to state a policy. Managers, supervisors, and systems must put it to work. The system can incorporate the policy decision in its related procedure. But then supervisors and managers must see that the provisions of the procedure are adhered to. Otherwise both the policy and the procedure will become useless.

If the person writing the procedure and the person designing the system understand policy, they can see that the necessary policy provisions are included. Then it is a question of hard-nosed, ordinary management discipline. The supervisor tells the employee, "Do it exactly as called for in the procedure." Without such discipline* throughout the company, the chief executive officer, like the skipper of a ship, although he turns the wheel will get no response at the rudder . . . and he cannot steer the ship.

In a poorly disciplined* organization, the supervisors and middle managers tolerate both policy and procedure deviations. Internal audit reports on this weakness are often ignored. This breakdown only happens because top management permits it.

 REMINDER: A management document is only a tool and to be effective a tool requires a tool *user.*

Internal auditors can assist management by reporting deviations from procedures or policies. But auditors need clearly written documents to serve as standards.

10. A POLICY CASE HISTORY

Let's consider a case history on policy. The subject, "Employee Parking," may not seem important to some executives but most employees think it is. Please remember: One of the characteristics of a policy is "that it tends to treat all people fairly."

People are interested in the company's parking facilities. To some men and women a personal parking stall means as much as a raise in pay. One of the ultimates in status is to have a private parking stall with the individual's name on it.

*To overcome such a serious fault, use the four rules of conduct offered in Richards & Magoon's little book *Discipline or Disaster.* See the recommended reading list.

As a company's outside document consultant I was asked to write a parking policy that management would "buy" and that would end the constant bickering and criticism from employees about their rights to park here or to park there. The parking facilities for the company's 2400 employees were quite good. And the one-story building was surrounded by paved parking areas.

We talked to a number of people who parked their cars during the two work shifts. Few were happy about the parking situation. One woman said, "You only get a stall in a good spot by favoritism . . . or through somebody you know." And a man said simply, "It isn't fair." A newly hired employee had a stall with his name on it next to that of the corporate treasurer. People who had to carry heavy materials and parts in and out of the plant during the day had to park out in the "boondocks." All lots were paved and had 10-foot-wide stalls on a diagonal pattern and concrete bumpers in the front. Six of the ten top executives had names on their stalls. The other four did not. Outside of the back lot, where anybody could park, some of the stalls were numbered. We found that the man handling the parking stall assignments was playing politics with them.

We determined that there were two aspects to consider in setting up an equitable parking policy for the company:

1.   Rank or status
2.   Work needs

Here is the policy draft that we wrote *after* going the full development route, including participation:

POLICY

No. 107
June 31, 19XX

Subject: Employee Parking

Personnel will notify employees who are assigned either numbered or named stalls. All other employees may park in the large back lot in any unnumbered or unnamed stall.

Front lot parking is reserved for the president, chairman of the board, vice-presidents, department heads, general supervisors, and general foremen.

Such classifications include managers on an equal level but with such titles as purchasing agent, chief of security, chief engineer, chief inspector, director of quality control, and chief draftsman. Front lot stalls that are individually assigned are numbered or named. Names on stalls will be limited to stalls assigned to company officers and department heads.

Visitors will park in the front lot at the direction of the guard at the gate. Applicants for employment will park in the front lot near the Personnel office. Each of these front lot stalls are marked either VISITORS or EMPLOYMENT. **Vendors and suppliers** also park in the west end of the front lot near the Materiel Department Entrance.

Stalls in the **west lot** are reserved for supervisors, foremen and for staff personnel reporting to general supervisors or higher.

The **east lot** stalls, located near the receiving dock, are to be used only for "work needs" parking. These numbered stalls are assigned to personnel based on their work requirements for going in or out of the plant on company business during the work shift. Only employees who must carry materials or parts in and out of the plant an average of 10 times a week or more will be assigned stalls in the east lot.

If work needs of an employee do change, the department head is to withdraw his or her east lot parking assignment by notifying Personnel.

Assigned parking stalls are identified by the assignee's name or by a number. If a stall is not marked, it is an "open" stall and may be used by the first driver who comes upon it.

Auto Identification. Each automobile that is parked in front, east, or west lot must be identified by a parking sticker. Stickers are not necessary for parking in the back (south) lot. Sticker colors apply as follows:

Front lot	Blue
East lot	Red
West lot	Green

Stall Assignment. Stalls are assigned only by a designated person in the office of the vice-president of Administration, and strictly in accordance with this policy. Plant Security is to be notified, in writing, of each assignment.

Security guards will patrol all lots on a 24-hour basis and will identify cars which are not parked in the proper lot.
Citations will be issued to individuals who park in stalls or areas to which they are not assigned. Copies of such citations will go to the department head concerned who will contact the employee's supervisor at once.

There are to be no exceptions to this policy. By order of:

> John Pryor, President
> RAMAC Electronics Co.

The company officers found that by developing this policy . . . and then *applying it* the problems were eliminated.

The security guard force of the organization was instructed to strictly enforce the sticker system set up to control parking. At first a number of citations were given out to violators who parked in stalls not assigned to them. Copies of their citations were sent to the department heads, who were required to notify the employee's supervisor. The violations dropped off at once.

Useful policy permits delegation. After a time one of the secretaries in the vice-president's office administered the parking policy. If someone asked her to deviate from the policy, she told that person, "No." If he insisted, she suggested that he see the vice-president. Nobody did. This was an example of a problem that was solved by:

1. A clear statement of policy

2. Policy based on two exact considerations:

    a. Status or rank in the organization

    b. Work needs

3. A specific person who was to administer the policy without exceptions

Another subject that concerns management is possible "conflict of interest." A chief of materiel issued this policy statement:

POLICY

Subject: Conflict of Interest

Representatives of the Company are reminded that one of the provisions for immediate discharge (contained in the company's disciplinary code) emphasizes that transactions between representatives of this Company and the vendors and suppliers who do business with the Company must at all times be conducted in a manner that is beyond criticism.

Any improper conduct or suggestion by a supplier to a representative of this Company aimed at influencing the selection of a supplier shall be promptly reported to the Chief of Materiel. Such improper conduct includes:

1. Any offer or acceptance of cash or its equivalent at any time under any circumstances.

2. Any other gift or gratuity when the circumstances surrounding the offer suggests possible improper conduct by the individual.

3. Other than ownership of investment stock in a publicly held corporation, having any interest, direct or indirect, in any organization which is engaged in or affected by contracts or orders placed by this Company.

11. WRITING POLICY

Profound or obscure writing will never make it on policy bulletins. The writing must make the subject "crystal clear" to *any* reader. Writing that is hard to understand will ruin the entire document program.

Clarity starts with the title on the bulletin. Call it what it is: POLICY. Keep the rest of the top area simple. Provide a place for the number and the effective date. If it is a revision, under the caption CANCELS write what number or numbers this replaces and the date of the previous issue. That's all. The "masthead" could look like this:

The company logo could go in the upper left corner. If the policy is departmental rather than corporate, the department name can go in the upper left.

The next item on a quality policy bulletin is the subject. Provide the caption *Subject:* at the top left, with a colon. Choose the subject carefully. Write only one policy on *one* subject. So the subject can be very exact. Here are some effective policy subjects:

Soliciting Funds from Employees	Inter-plant Transfers
Gratuities from Vendors	Time off for
	a. Voting
Conflicts of Interest	*b.* Jury Duty
Blood Bank Donations	Organization Changes
Classified Documents	Data Security
	Employment of Relatives
Vacations	Entry During Non-Working Hours
Sick Leave	
Personal Mail at the Office	

Undoubtedly much policy in an organization is unwritten. As such it is not very useful. Policy that exists only in the mind of one man or one woman cannot be communicated to policy users. The unwritten policy dies with the removal of the person. So such policies are not as enduring as everything in a corporation should be. A corporation is a deathless entity, an "individual" in the eyes of the law. It does not die because some of its employees go away or die.

There is only one way you can state policy so that it is useful. WRITE IT. You can't make a policy decision clear to other people . . . and often not even to yourself, if you fail to write it.

All of us are interested in personnel policies. Here is a typical personnel policy:

Sick Leave. After you have completed six months of full-time, continuous service, you will be eligible to receive a maximum of seven days of sick leave with pay, each year. The eligible year starts from the hire date. Your sick leave pay will begin on the second day of absence due to accident or illness, but such incapacity to work does require a doctor's certificate. Your sick leave benefits do not accumulate from one calendar year to the next.

Would that policy be clear to the person reading it? We think it would. Notice that the writing is directed to the person, to each employee, in the "you" mode: "After you have . . . you will be eligible . . . your sick leave benefits . . ."

To be useful, policy must be written clearly and distributed correctly.

Behind that simple statement staff and management people have put in considerable thought. They considered the pros and cons on the subject of sick leave. They asked: How many days to give? Should it be carried over to the following calendar year? What does our competition for good employees in this area do about sick leave?

Writing a policy has another important advantage. Because it can be examined and compared, one policy is unlikely to conflict with or contradict another policy on the same subject.

QUESTION: Is a written policy a sure-fire means of communicating?

ANSWER: Certainly not. But as one author put it, "Yes, I admit that even the written word on a policy statement is not distortion proof. But it will suffer far less from distortion than will its oral counterpart."

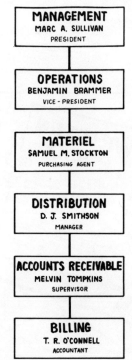

The scalar-chain of command is necessary for management control, but it is not an effective channel of communication.

Oral policy must filter down, through the links in the chain of command. And repeated studies of communication accuracy through that chain shows that 70 to 80 percent of the accuracy of a message will have been lost in the "journey" between the president and the rank-and-file employee.

Use this 10-point check list to help you write the policy:

1. Put your statement on a bulletin that says at the masthead exactly what the bulletin is . . . POLICY.

2. It has a carefully thought out subject such as: *Control of Plant Visitors.*

3. If appropriate, the situation in which the policy is to be applied can be spelled out. Just say "Situation."

4. Next spell out the body of the policy. Write each sentence simply. EXAMPLE: We allow discounts only if the invoice payment reaches accounts receivable in the first ten days of the following month.

5. Tells exactly what *should be done*. This is the positive aspect of a policy.

6. Tell exactly what *not* to do. This is the negative or "fencing in" aspect of a policy.

7. Are any exceptions permitted? Under what circumstances? Who can make an exception?

8. Approving authority of the policy. This will consist of a typewritten name, with an executive's title such as president, and his or her personal signature above the typewritten name.

   a. If a policy applies only within one department, the department head signs it. If it applies to the entire corporation, the chief executive officer (CEO) signs it.

9. The document will have a number. Assign the numbers sequentially, one and up. Do not use any significant numbering scheme.

10. It will have an effective date or a revision date.

Perhaps one of the simplest and most effective policies is the one originated long ago in retailing: "You must be satisfied or your money back."

Now let's look at another situation and problem, and the policy statement that helped the manager solve the problem. *Situation:* A senior accountant in the general accounting section of a large corporation went to his manager and said:

> Mr. Murray, *I am sick and tired* of the people in the department coming to me from time to time asking for gifts for this and for contributions for that. Somebody is going away, somebody got sick, somebody is having a baby, somebody is getting married and somebody is quitting. Other people are peddling products to other employees on company time. The last solicitation really got to me. Somebody wanted to collect funds in order to send Mrs. Hamilton's granddaughter, Susie Clifton, to the bowling championship over in Kansas City. In the last three months, I have had to pony up $123. And that's got to come out of something that my family needs. Can't you put a stop to it?

The man expressed a need for a policy on "Solicitations." Other employees had complained but not to the manager. Together the accountant and his manager developed a memo (they didn't think to put it on a policy bulletin form). It read as follows:

We've had a number of complaints from employees that they are receiving constant solicitation for funds or gifts, sometimes several in one week. I think you will agree that if an employee doesn't feel that he or she wants to continue making these contributions, it is that employee's right to decline.

We discussed this matter with Mr. Haney in Personnel and with his advice we developed the following policy: If the majority of the employees in the department want to sign a petition requesting, in a special case, that they be given an approval to solicit money or gifts, before asking for signatures, bring the petition to the supervisor for consideration. If the supervisor does not give specific approval, and/or less than the majority of the people sign the petition, soliciting money or gifts from any employee in any section is hereby forbidden. "Solicitation" is not limited to money or gifts. It includes the selling of articles or items in the company during business hours. This is strictly forbidden. Any employee who does so will receive an official first reprimand, which will go in the employee's personnel file. If employees want to contact each other after hours, such as on the parking lot, that is their individual right and privilege. Any employee who violates the provisions of this policy after the effective date, will be subject to disciplinary action.

The manager distributed copies of his memo to each employee in the section and put one copy on a nearby bulletin board. The writing style wasn't the best, but people understood it.

12. DISTRIBUTING POLICY

Let's say that now you have a clearly written policy, a useful management document. The process of developing it was triggered (started) by a real need at the operating level. Alternative solutions were developed and considered. One was accepted, carefully written, coordinated, revised, approved, and reproduced.

Now *who* should get a copy? As they say, "A good question." And usually not well answered. The distribution scheme can be sloppy, with policy statements going to people who *don't* need them and completely missing the people who *do* need them.

The entire process of management communication could founder at this point . . . on distribution. You may ask, "Why not send policy to the same people who get copies of statements of work and organization charts?" No. The distribution plan of each document must be thought out. If you have a policy on "Traveling on Company Business," would you consider it good distribution to send it to hundreds of supervisors who never travel on company business? They have no "need to know."

The key is just that . . . the need to know. We've referred to the developer of management documents as the "Management Documents Officer." That is not a title for just anyone. It means a person who *knows* or who knows how to *find out* about the real needs to know in all parts of the organization.

While your policies may now be scattered and in various forms
including memos, one "package" of policies will probably already exist . . . personnel policies. These may now be contained
in an employee booklet covering such subjects as employment,
working hours, probation, full-time and part-time work, over-
time, vacations, sick leave, and wages and salaries. These, of
course, go to all employees. To distribute other policies correctly, I recommend that you classify your company's policies into
logical "bundles" such as:

1. Corporate or universal policies. Most personnel
   policies fall into this category.

2. Departmental or work needs policies. Purchasing
   policies, accounting policies, and sales policies are
   in this classification.

3. Specialized policies. These would cover subjects
   like:

   Traveling on Company Business
   Engaging the Services of a Consultant
   Company Business Cards
   Expense Accounts
   Conflicts of Interest
   Business Shows

The masthead titles (at the top of the document) can vary like
these examples:

1. CORPORATE POLICIES
2. PERSONNEL POLICIES
3. ACCOUNTING POLICIES
4. MANAGEMENT POLICIES

These last may be so specialized that they are not needed by
most employees. Each category can be numbered simply . . . one
and up. Since the personnel bulletins are specialized corporate
policies, these bulletin numbers could have a prefix such as
PERS-.

Various distribution schemes have been used. All corporate policies could go to everyone shown on the organization chart. Other lists are titled "All Department Heads and Supervisors" . . . or "All Manual Holders." Do see what lists are available now. One of these lists can be a *starter* upon which you could build your policy reader list. To use "wholesale" lists that already exist is one way to distribute policy. But do study each list; don't stop at the title. Who is really on the list?

Think about this: If it is important that an employee know and apply a specific policy, his or her adherence to that policy is not possible if the policy statement doesn't reach that individual. It is better to have a few too many copies distributed than too few.

Since you will know what procedure (system) incorporates a specific policy, the procedure may be all that some individuals need. Good judgment, based on a thorough knowledge of "the need to know," must be applied here. Do check the organization charts and do study the statements of work. They will help.

When you're certain that one specific group of maybe 15 people has a need to know, but you are not sure of the needs of individuals within that group, use the "information copy" technique. Send two copies of the policy to the supervisor. One is on white paper and it is punched. This goes into the manual binder at once. The second copy is on green paper, is not punched, but is to circulate within the group of employees. This copy has large outline letters on it, set on the diagonal, INFORMATION COPY. At the bottom is this notice: "This copy is for circulation only. It will not be maintained. Do not punch. Do not place in a binder."

Does each group have a bulletin board? The circulation copy could be pinned there. Show a take down and destroy date of 10 days beyond the issue date.

13. MAINTAINING YOUR POLICIES

The base of your maintenance work is a folder for each policy bulletin . . . including papers that make up a "case history" on that specific policy.

When your executives decided to follow a definite policy in relation to a problem, they probably did so only after they considered several alternatives.

However, as time goes by . . . months and years later, the reasons behind the decision (that resulted in the published policy) tend to fade in the memories of men and women. So the case history folder becomes a permanent memory . . . a type of *systems* memory.

What goes in the folder? These items:

1. Your original report that led to the present policy. This includes any alternatives and a description of the situation at the time.

2. The "reasons why" the executives selected the alternative. This may be a copy of the executive staff's minutes.

3. Two copies of the final policy bulletin.

4. One copy of any earlier versions of the policy.

5. One copy of the related procedure, the one that is based on the policy.

6. Any other documents, such as memos, that relate to the policy or to the situation.

7. Departments and people who are affected by the policy.

8. The names (and their departments) that you contacted during the participation phase.

9. What distribution list you used.

Write the bulletin number and the subject on the index tab of the folder. File the folder permanently. Sooner or later someone will want to change the policy. If so, take out the folder. Does the suggester want to go back to an older policy, one that you abandoned years ago? Or does the suggester think that you should select one of the other alternatives? These were considered and rejected earlier. Has the situation changed?

Now your systematic memory (the case history file folder) becomes a valuable tool. The papers containing all the original information are assets.

Set up a system for maintaining your management documents. Pivot the system around a case history work folder.

You don't want to start the study all over again. It's too costly to do so. At the same time you must encourage people to suggest policy changes that they feel will benefit the organization.

People out on the operations floor or in the offices can be the first to recognize that a policy, once a real help, has now become a hindrance.

When a conscientious worker sees that a policy (developed and issued five years previously) is no longer working to the best advantage of the organization, encourage that employee to point this out.

If the person doing the work has no voice in policy development or suggested changes . . . he will take one of two courses:

1. He will tend to ignore the policy and do what he
    (or she) thinks is right. This new direction may
    not lead to the organization's goals.

2. He will follow the policy even though it obviously
    is not in the organization's best interest.

The object is to let people give thoughtful consideration to
any suggested change and do so easily. If the policy worked well
at first and now really needs revision, probably the *situation* has
changed. That's why you preserved a description of the original
situation in the case history folder. Policy is apt to change more
slowly than any other management document, but it can and
does change.

Should it be revised? If so, now you go through the same process that you did in originating the policy. However, now you can
move rather quickly. Neither you nor the suggester make the
policy decision. The *responsible executives do!* You'd write up the
proposed revision and coordinate it with others who are involved. (Your folder will remind you of who was involved originally.) Then submit the revised draft to the approving authority.
And of course you'll include notes on the reasons for the
change. Some developers point out the changes on a copy of the
current policy statement.

If your policies are not changed when they should be, people
will tend to deviate from the policy provisions. Then the document begins to lose its value.

Set up a systems channel so that such suggestions can come
directly to you. Check at once with the supervisor. Then go to
the person. DO NOT VIOLATE THE CHAIN OF COM-
MAND. Diplomacy is the key word in this situation.

14. SUMMARY ON POLICY

Policy is not a vague, will-o-the-wisp idea. But it is widely misunderstood and mixed in people's minds with other management
documents. Therefore it is poorly used. Yet policy can be (and is

in a few companies) a powerful management tool, a "document to manage by."

To be useful policy must be written. The writing is always in simple English. Policy is a directional decision . . . "If we go this way we'll gain the most advantages and suffer the least disadvantages."

Policy achieves quality only when you develop it in partnership with the men and women who will use it. To maintain that quality, be alert at all times to the need for a policy revision.

Initiative at the operating level is important to every organization's welfare. Policy can permit the intelligent exercise of individual initiative at the operating level, but it will also prevent that initiative from leading the organization *away* from its selected goals. There are practical limits to the exercise of initiative by people on the "firing line."

A body of well-thought-out policy statements, distributed to those who are to use them, supplies the organization with codes of conduct whereby employee activities can be governed and controlled.

One large company that deals heavily overseas developed a policy in regard to bribes. The policy was made clear to each executive and to each employee. Each employee must read the company's guidelines: "Political contributions, pay-offs, bribes or any other questionable payments are strictly prohibited." Employees sign cards that they clearly understand that any departure from these guidelines (policies) can result in dismissal.

Finally a word about quantity and quality. Do not develop so many policy documents that you can't maintain them. Policies relating to personnel matters can be packaged separately. All policies must be maintained . . . must always be dependable guides for the men and women who make dozens of operating decisions daily.

Chapter 5

PROCEDURES

Management's ultimate responsibility is to get action through the employees . . . and to get *results*. Organization charts, statements of work, and policies are basic documents. They reflect fundamental management decisions but, in themselves, do not get results.

The action patterns in the organization are dynamic and, of course, lead to the necessary daily *results* such as: goods sold, articles designed, products manufactured, money collected, items shipped, services rendered, control exercised, materials purchased, and materials transported.

Behind these activities are the people who do the work . . . engineers, salesmen, factory workers, buyers, accountants, shipping clerks. While each individual must do his or her work well, the key requirement is for *teamwork* . . . of people working together to achieve finally not just an individual's result but the bigger, *together* result.

So a fourth document falls into the category of "documents to manage by" . . . the *procedure*.

To consider the procedure we must turn our attention to those numerous lateral relationships that stretch between and among departments, sections, and many people. It is these "horizontal" action channels that weld a dozen or a hundred people into a single-purpose team. Each person or each group may be a work specialist but it takes a combination of people to get every important *result*!

126

1. WHAT IS A PROCEDURE?

Three terms need clarification: *system, procedure* and *computer*. Just because computer manufacturers say that their machines are systems doesn't make them so. The term "system" is an effective selling tool, so people with sales responsibility use it generously.

There are hundreds of types of systems, so our type of system is best called a *management* system. And it is a TOTALITY. The system is an *action getting plan.* The plan includes a channel of action, data handling tools (including the computer), procedures, printed forms, files of all types (including data bases), programs (instructions for machines), task outlines (instructions for people), methods, and regular reports. All together these make up a system . . . a *management* system. Observe, please, that the procedure is just one element in the totality that we call a system.

The *procedure* is a written description of the action sequences of the system. Thus it is a road map, essential for any lengthy journey. We will use the term in that single sense . . . a written description of the system. Here is an example:

PROCEDURE

Subject: Setting Up a Contractual Budget

Who		**Does What**
Budget Secretary	1.	Receives Sales Order Form 779 from Contracts Administration.
	2.	Stamps Sales Order with department time and date stamp.
	3.	Logs Sales Order number on bid record card and on Estimating Form 421.
	4.	Gives Sales Order to statistical clerk.
Statistical Clerk	5.	Pulls bid folder from bid file and stamps with sales order stamp.
	6.	Attaches Sales Order to folder and gives to budget analyst.

Who	Does What
Budget Analyst	7. Studies Sales Order and compares to the original bid. Makes out Budget Estimate, Form 926, and gives to statistical clerk.
	7a. If Sales Order shows price, writes "Copy Cost Analysis Detail" on Sales Order.
Statistical Clerk	8. Types enough copies of "budget" for distribution as shown at lower left corner of Form 926.
	8a. Checks Sales Order. If budget analyst has written "Copy Cost Analysis Detail" on it, removes cost analysis from bid folder and obtains copies for distribution.
	9. Returns Sales Order, bid folder, contractual budget (a typed rough draft), and copy of cost analysis to budget analyst.
Budget Analyst and Secretary	10. Proof, as a team, all detail on typed copies of budget. If correct, both initial the first copy.
Budget Analyst	11. Checks Sales Order for any still needed cost analysis requirements.
	12. Returns to statistical clerk.
Statistical Clerk	13. Distributes budget and cost analysis copies.
	14. Attaches typed draft of budget in the bid folder.
	15. Files the updated bid folder in the Sales Order locked file.

In that segment of team action there are three players or "actors": the budget secretary, the statistical clerk, and the budget analyst. The sequence ends with an updated contractual budget file. That is the *result* of the three-person activity of setting up a contractual budget.

In most organizations there are hundreds, even thousands, of such short cycle systems and the procedures that reflect them. Unfortunately most procedures are not that clear.

In one company of 6,500 employees we counted the published procedures in use. There were 446 of them. Some described the teamwork that individuals performed within a single department. Others linked the activities of departments. The totals of procedures used in the departments were as follows:

Department or Function	Quantity of Procedures	Department or Function	Quantity of Procedures
Personnel	24	Production	45
Purchasing	18	Corporate Research	5
Marketing	17	Distribution	21
Systems and data processing	131	Merchandising	24
Treasury	11	Administration	25
Legal and public affairs	7	Accounting and Finance	118

Perhaps two percent of those procedures (9) would reflect the company's "big show" systems. We'll explain the meaning of the term "big show" shortly. We bring it up here because all key executives should *know* those few key procedures so well that they can recite the sequences without opening a procedures manual.

2. QUALITY OF PROCEDURES

It is our observation that most procedures, like other management documents, are not top quality. Some are clumsy attempts at combining several documents into one . . . to "reduce paper work." Such procedures contain elements of policy, individual instructions, explanations, and statements of responsibility.

The poor quality starts with the name of the document itself. Few are called "procedures." Instead strange, legalistic terms predominate, such as *standard practice, methods bulletin, administrative standards, office directives, executive instructions, supervisory guides,* or *standard operating procedures.*

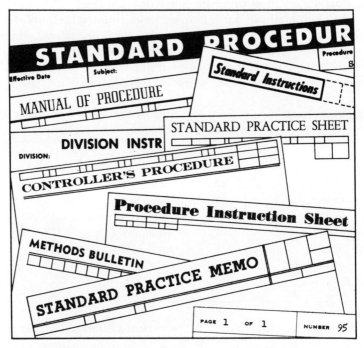

The usual documents jungle does not provide a harmonious set of documents to manage by.

Most of such obtuse terms really mean a write-up that should be called a procedure. But the "how to proceed" idea was further fogged by the practice of using initials to represent obscure titles such as SPB to represent "Standard Practice Bulletin." Other initials are:

MOP	SM	SPI
SI	MB	SIP
SBP	SP	SPIB
SPP		

And if that wasn't enough to downgrade the value of a vital management document, the writing itself doesn't exactly permit speed reading.

STANDARD PRACTICE INSTRUCTION

Subject: Handling Transfers and Budget Adjustments of Personnel

It shall be company policy and practice to transfer employees from one department to another when the work needs so require such transfer. Transfers of personnel shall not be made without prior adjustment of the current personnel budgets and work-load records maintained currently in the accounting and finance division, budget and planning section.

The personnel department shall have the authority to secure the receiving department's supervisory signature on all transfers which are to be made between overhead and productive departments. Personnel shall set the effective date of transfer, and this shall be added to Form 457, Transfer Request, in the space provided. Copies 2 and 3 shall be sent to the department receiving personnel so transferred, while copy 1 will be filed.

All budget and work-load records shall be adjusted from a copy of Form 457 which shall be sent to the budget and planning section of Accounting and Finance.

Approval of both the releasing and receiving departmental supervisors shall be necessary before the request for a transfer can be effective. The releasing department's personnel records, but not the Personnel Department folder, shall be sent to the receiving department, along with their copy of Form 457. All other affected personnel records shall be posted to reflect the transfer, particularly in the receiving department, as receiving department records must be up-to-date and each employee shall be currently charged to the correct burden or cost-center account. It is a company policy to keep such employee's record folder in a locked personnel records cabinet. Only supervisors shall have access to, or may refer to these records.

You *could* understand that procedure after a bit of studying and rereading. But the same information can be arranged in a more readable form, such as:

PROCEDURE

Subject: Personnel Transfers

Actor	Action
Releasing Supervisor	1. Completes Form 457, "Transfer Request."

Actor	Action
	2. Sends both copies to Budgets and Planning.
Budgets and Planning	3. Adjusts budget and workload records.
	4. Sends both copies of Form 457 to Personnel.
Personnel	5. Secures receiving department supervisor's signature.
	6. Adds effective date of transfer to Form 457 and:
	6a. Sends copy 2 to receiving department.
	6b. Files copy 1.
	7. Notifies releasing department of effective date by telephone.
	8. Places file copy of Form 457 in personnel folder.
Releasing Supervisor	9. Delivers department personnel records folder to receiving department.
	10. Posts department personnel records to reflect the change.
Receiving Supervisor	11. Files employee records folder in locked personnel records cabinet.

Easy to read? To see who does what? And in what sequence? Is the teamplay clear in this employee inter-department transfer system? You're looking at the *Playscript** type of procedure.

The ordinary procedure does not follow a standard layout. Some procedures are sprinkled with "big words" or mysterious initials. When analyzed, some procedures are really covering

Playscript is covered in more detail in the author's book *The New Playscript Procedure*. See the page on recommended reading.

two or three subjects. If there is a pattern that reflects teamwork actions, it isn't readily apparent to the reader. The write-up does not accurately describe the related system. Here is one such procedure:

STANDARD PRACTICE BULLETIN

Subject: Disbursement Documents for Handling Cash

PURPOSE: This procedure and policy covers the usage in processing of cash disbursement vouchers, form 971-B. It has been written to provide a system and a means for the payment and control of bills and invoices that are not properly supported by a purchase order or other authorization. A cash disbursement voucher is a request and will be authorized for the issuance of a check only after the required approvals have been obtained.

POLICY: Normally all material, labor, and/or services performed by persons outside the Company shall be contracted for by the purchasing department. The only exceptions to this rule are where authority has been delegated to another individual or department by the purchasing department or the function is one that is not normally handled by them such as the payment of special advisory fees, etc.

Cash disbursement vouchers shall be used to effect payment of the Company's obligations that have not been previously covered by a purchase order. On freight, rent, or on utilities bills, purchase orders are not required. Invoices for books, magazines, newspapers and periodicals shall be sent to the central library for payment. In this case see SPB 181.

Individuals requesting payment of the above nature or others not covered by a purchase order shall hand print a cash disbursement voucher form in five parts, completing all sections and secure the signature of the authorized department head in the "department head approval" box on the form. Copies will be distributed to general accounting, the payee, and one copy filed alphabetically by payee.

It shall be the duty of general accounting to verify the account number and to forward the voucher to individuals indicated in paragraphs 8 and 9 for their approval. Travel expense items such as hotel bills, car rentals, and airline invoices shall be charged to the employee advanced account, rather than directly to the departmental travel expenses. In the case of dues and contributions, these shall be approved by the treasurer or the chairman of the dues and contributions committee and handled through the cash disbursement procedure.

All cash disbursement vouchers originating in any division or department must be approved by the local controller or his or her designee, and individual cash disbursements in excess of $10,000 shall also be approved by the corporate controller or his or her designee. The corporate controller or his or her designee may approve emergency division or department cash disbursement vouchers in the absence of the divisional controller.

Any approved and vouchered CDV's for the treasurer or treasury checks shall be forwarded to the assistant treasurer's office along with supporting papers and transmittals to be mailed with the check. Always include the third copy of the CDV form. In cases where a CDV is issued, and it results in a duplicate payment of the UED accounts payable department, it shall forward a CDV typed in red and indicate that prior payment has been made to the originator of the duplicated payment of CDV asking him for a letter of explanation.

Many procedures provide lots of information but they fail to tell each "actor" how to proceed to get results.

Such procedures can be described as talking more or less "around and about a subject." The writing styles are different and the presentation patterns vary. One writer's procedure may contradict what another writer says in another procedure.

Another weakness of ordinary procedures is that the writer does not distinguish between instructions for one person and in explaining how two or more people can work together effectively. The emphasis on strong teamwork is lacking.

By recognizing the difference between a procedure and a "task outline," the author can "peel off" detailed information of value only to an individual. (More on task outlines later in this chapter.) Which brings us back to a practical concept that we've mentioned before:

 Design each type of document to achieve ONE PURPOSE!

3. THE ACTION PATTERN

If you look for it, you can find an action pattern in any system. And that is what the useful (quality) procedure must bring out.

The word *procedure* means just one thing: How people are to proceed to work together. Note the word "people." It includes more than one person . . . two or more. Again we see the idea of teamwork.

Naturally you want the procedure, as a management document, to do the best possible job for your organization. Why not? To insure that desirable quality in your procedures, do these things:

1. Accept the "single document for a single purpose" concept.

2. Immediately scrap all the funny old names such as "standard instruction bulletins." Call the document a *procedure*.

3. Write the action steps in their logical sequence.

4. Limit the write up to one sensible cycle of action, such as from customer's order to shipping.

5. Write all procedures in a simple format.

The procedure style that meets those requirements is called *Playscript* and the author developed it decades ago. Today it is the procedures standard in thousands of companies and organizations. We'll explain *Playscript* more fully a little later, but since it incorporates a number of systems and procedures *concepts,* we'll consider a few of those concepts next.

PROCEDURE – *THE WAY TO PROCEED*

The procedure's job is to help each person see what his job is and how that single job fits into the team-work plan.

4. SYSTEMS AND PROCEDURES CONCEPTS

Without a grasp of the concepts upon which it is based, you may look upon the *Playscript* procedure as merely a format. But it is a procedure writing technique that incorporates a half dozen practical systems concepts:

1. A procedure is a written document that reflects a system.

2. Each system is a plan that enables people to work together.

3. In each system a limited number of people will participate. These are the "actors."

4. Some systems are more vital to the organization than are others. These are the "big show" systems. In each organization there are one or two "big show" activities. These represent the reason why the organization itself exists. All other activities are support for the big show or big shows.

5. In every system there is a logical, easy-to-understand sequence of action steps.

6. Systems transactions flow through an invisible but traceable systems channel.

7. Each transaction requires a trigger (start), some essential processing, and finally a result.

8. Systems are plans for cooperative effort among people. The machines people use are not systems. They are systems *tools*.

9. There is an identifiable "main line" in each system and most transactions travel along that line.

10. The main line must be simple and straight, so that transactions can move to completion quickly.

11. A minority of transactions (exceptions) must run on "side tracks." These are to be identified and provided for *only* after the main line is cleared of all obstructions.

12. A system's major purpose is to get a result that is obtainable only by people taking specific actions.

13. The action aspect of the system is supported by memory or records (data bases, etc.). Information stored in memory can be reused in the action cycle, or it can be used as a basis for generating reports on results. These reports can be "hard copy" (paper) or in the form of a data cluster presented on a cathode ray tube (on a terminal).

14. People get the results by playing individual roles within the teamwork plan. Such "actors" are named by their official job titles, not personal names.

15. The key procedures and the key systems that they describe are the "big show" procedures. Every executive must know intimately the sequences of his or her eight to ten key procedures.

5. THE PLAYSCRIPT PROCEDURE

The *Playscript* type of procedure incorporates all the foregoing concepts, with stress on the concept of the main line, the systems cycle, and the systems channel for processing data.

In using *Playscript* the writer recognizes that things don't just happen, but *that people make them happen!* The people who play a role in each systems cycle are the actors in a slice of human dramatic action.

The procedure's two outside brackets are the *trigger* and the *result* . . . the beginning and the end. Consider the system that people call "purchasing" and the related procedure. Some of the people who take part are located in the purchasing department, but not all of them are. The process of purchasing or buying usually starts elsewhere. The action starts when someone or something (a computer, perhaps) identifies a need. EXAMPLE: A man in the stock room, while processing his stock withdrawal slips (the program in the computer can do this), gets a new inventory balance. He sees that the quantity of one part has reached the "low stock point" so he originates a purchase requisition. These are the systematic actions:

1. (Trigger) Someone or something (perhaps the computer) recognizes there is a need to buy an item because the stock is low.

2. This person (or machine) launches the purchasing action by filling out a requisition (an action getting form).

3. The buyer, in response to the requisition, places the order with the supplier by issuing a purchase order.

4. After receiving the order, the supplier ships the item ordered.

5. When the goods arrive a worker on the receiving dock checks in the order.

6. (Result) A stock clerk places the new supply of the item on the stockroom shelf.

There you have it, (1) a "trigger" reflecting a need and (2) finally a "result" . . . the replenishment of that low-stock item. That completes the purchasing systems cycle.

Select a logical systems cycle and pin down the 2 brackets of the system . . . the trigger and the result.

Obviously in any organization people use a whole network of systems. Therefore they need a network of procedures that accurately reflect those systems so that the participants can understand the action pattern.

How long should a systems cycle be? There is no arbitrary length. It is up to the judgment of the analyst to decide whether he is describing a logical package of work.

In a very large purchasing system, the cycle may not cover the action from the need (trigger) to the replenishment in inventory (result). The analyst may break that large cycle into many smaller cycles such as:

1. The requisition cycle
2. Quotation and bid cycle
3. The purchasing cycle (placing the order)
4. Receiving cycle
5. Inspection and accepting cycle
6. The stock replacement cycle
7. Paying cycle

The last, of course, is called the accounts payable system (or procedure). The purchasing cycle and the paying cycle are related. The paying cycle cannot be activated until the purchasing cycle is complete. People don't pay for what they don't get.

The word *logical* is important. Some systems cycles can be very short, with only three or four processing steps between the trigger and the result. The earlier example (of the procedure setting up the contractual budget) represented a short cycle. In another situation the analyst may feel that a logical system cycle (and the procedure that reflects it) should include 40 or 50 processing steps. We have seen logical cycles, that we would agree *are* sensible packages of work, that included more than 100 processing steps.

However, the average systems cycle should not include more than about *25 steps*. Now let's look at an example of one "big show" procedure with 31 steps and written in *Playscript:*

PROCEDURE

Subject: Order Entry

Performed By   **Action**

Sales
Representative

1. Obtains order in the form of a
    customer's purchase order, a broker's
    purchase order, or by personal contact
    with customer or broker.

2. Reviews order to determine
    availability of product, and/or whether
    to accept or reject the order.

    2a. Contacts customer or
         broker if the order is to
         be rejected or if any
         coordination is required.

3. Records the buyer's name in the
    "Customer Order" log.

4. Prepares an "Enter Contract Only,"
    Form 786-C, for accepted orders.

5. Assigns a contract number, with the
    sales district prefix, and records the
    customer's name in the contract
    number assignment book.

6. Gives the order and the contract
    description form to the district's order
    entry clerk.

Order Entry
Clerk

7. Prepares a "Sales Contract,"
    Form 410-M, for each order and
    enters the market price and the date
    of shipment. (The market price on the
    date that the shipment is made will
    apply.)

8. Distributes the five copies
    of the contract as called for on Form
    410-M.

Performed By	**Action**
Order Entry Clerk	8a. Sends first copy to customer for his signature and returns other copies to buyer, to broker, to sales department, and to sales statistics.

9. Assigns an order number for all orders and records the customer's name in the "Order Number Log Book."

10. Prepares an "order blank" in five copies.

11. Determines the date of shipment.

    11a. If for export orders, requests the customer to send shipping instructions. Assigns a lot number and provides any special instructions.

12. Makes necessary entries in the "Shipping Schedule for Week of " book.

13. Records the orders in the shipments for month of _____ log.

    13a. Prepares a "Customer Shipping Schedule" showing the order number, shipping date, and transportation mode and ship to point.

14. Pulls corresponding Customer Information Card for each order.

15. Prepares "Factory Shipping Order" using data obtained from the Customer Information Card and the order blank.

16. Distributes the "Factory Shipping Order" as called for on the form.

17. Refiles the Customer Information Card and attaches the Order Blank to the

Performed By   **Action**

pink copy to be sent to Credit
Department.

18. Takes next action when the "Daily
Production, Inventory and Loading
Report" arrives with the forms set.
(Form 368 will show what cars have
been loaded and shipped.)

19. Removes the verification card
attached to the form set, then
prepares a separate "Shipped Sheet"
for each product.

20. Records on the blue copy of the
"Factory Shipping Order" (FSO) the
car number and the seal numbers
from the Daily Production Report.

21. Forwards blue copy of FSO to Traffic
Department.

Traffic
Department   22. Prepares Bill of Lading (B/L)
and records weight on FSO from the
weigh ticket.

23. Forwards FSO, B/L, and weigh ticket to
Sales Department.

Order Entry
Clerk   24. Checks the FSO off the Daily Report
of Shipments.

25. Records Shipping information in the
contracts book, the export book, and
in product records book.

26. Checks freight on the FSO.

27. Calculates the billed price per ton and
records on the FSO.

Note: The price per ton equals the
market price per ton plus
freight per ton. See task outline
No. 9, titled, "Calculating
Freight Tons and Rates."

Performed By	**Action**
Order Entry Clerk	28. Pulls billing cards and prepares a Billing Data Sheet, Form 403-K.
	29. Forwards to Accounting the Billing Data Sheet, the Billing Card, the Blue copy of the FSO, the B/L (three copies), and the weigh ticket, the original order blank and related correspondence, and "return receipt."
	30. Sets up customer pending file for the return receipt.
	30a. If receipt is not received in five days, contacts accounting.
	31. Receives the Sales Department (goldenrod) copy of the invoice, with attached documents from Accounting.

Notice that at step 27, the procedure refers to a "task outline," a document used for detailed individual instruction, in this case, information on how to "Calculate Freight Tons and Rates." By using task outlines the procedure developer relieves the procedure from carrying detailed instruction that is of concern only to one individual. Thus the procedure performs its basic function of describing the system . . . which is also the picture of the *team* play.

A task outline, of course, has only one actor. But the document does use many *Playscript* features. It is written sequentially, each sentence starts with a "work word" (present tense verb), and the work actions are in logical (normal) sequence. Here is an example of a task outline:

TASK OUTLINE

Task No. 17

Subject: Preparing Student's Work for Instructors

Work of: Registrar's Clerk

1. Upon receipt of work from the mail room, pull student records from visi-record file.

2. Arrange student's report envelopes numerically so that instructor will receive each class in order, from low to high.

3. Pull all project report(s) from the envelopes.

4. Staple report copies, together with any student-prepared exhibits or examples.

5. Destroy envelopes.

6. Stamp top page with grade stamp in lower right-hand corner.

7. Prepare instructor's "Time Record" in duplicate, filling in:

   7a. Instructor's name.

   7b. Date.

   7c. Course work to be corrected, by lesson numbers.

8. Show number of projects given to each instructor on the time record.

9. Distribute lesson projects to assigned instructors.

10. Record number of student's lesson reports classified by course number on the "Distribution Sheet." (These will be used to prepare the monthly report for the director of instruction.)

11. Give work to instructor or mail if instructor is out of town.

12. File duplicate time record in instructor's "pay envelope."

13. Attach original of the time record to the total stack of work for each instructor.

Both the procedure and the task outline have a "main line." Write that main line first. Then go back and provide for the "side tracks" or exceptions. Show the exception by indentation and a small letter suffix, such as:

   9a. If the request is not approved, give reasons for disapproval and return to requester.

6. TOP MANAGEMENT'S ROLE

Shouldn't the group of documents that people use to manage by be in harmony one with the other? Many of them are not. They

are put out piecemeal, by different authorities, in all kinds of
formats (memos, frequently) and at different times. The result is
a "document jungle."

One cure for such a waste is a reasonable interest in all the key
documents by the top eight or ten executives. They don't need
to be concerned with the hundreds or even thousands of such
documents. But it would be no mental strain for the president
and his immediate subordinates to know intimately:

1. The five or six major procedures (covering "big
    show" activities).

2. The dozen most important policies.

3. The six to eight top organization charts.

4. The matching statements of work.

5. The ten or twelve major action forms (those used
    in the "big show" areas).

NOTE ONE: To the document developer: Provide a small se-
            lection of such documents to each top officer.
            Put them in an attractive, special binder. Ar-
            range to keep each binder up to date.

NOTE TWO: To the president and to the vice-presidents:
            The only way you will get a harmonious set of
            document tools is to have a capable documents
            officer pull them all together for you and keep
            them that way. Otherwise your organization will
            continue to be burdened with its document jun-
            gle.

7. RELATIVES OF THE PROCEDURE

Now let's consider the procedure's "relatives." We discussed its
detailed "cousin," the task outline. Another close relation, practically a partner to the procedure, is the action (printed) form.
Transactions move on forms such as purchase orders, sales order, production or shop orders, invoices, and voucher checks
. . . just to name a few.

Many of the action sentences in the procedure include the name and number of the form the "actor" is to use. A policy statement may say that, "A newly hired employee is entitled to XX days of paid vacation after completing one year of full-time service." That's the *what* of a policy. How about the *how*? The procedure provides the how information, stating that, "The supervisor fills out Form 69, Vacation Request, and sends it to personnel records, etc."

Exactly what a clerk in the personnel records does with the request could be the subject of a detailed task outline.

The organization chart and its related statement of work both show the organization's structure and spell out the permanent work assignments. You could think of those two documents as presenting a vertical work list. Then it is the "main line" procedure that weaves across those vertical lists but does so horizontally. The procedure picks up, as it were, the duties listed in a static form and fits them into the dynamic team play . . . into the procedure and into the system that it represents.

Part of the company's authority pattern (often an approval matrix) will be found in the various procedures. But we have seen authority documents that did not fit the approval patterns as spelled out in the procedures. Members of management must recognize that the various documents are not isolated . . . but are a harmonious set of management tools.

8. SUMMARY

A quality procedure is a *written* document that provides the reader with a view of the team play or system. Most procedures do not provide such a picture and are not carefully thought out. They name a subject and talk around and about that subject. They are hard to write, hard to read, are nonsequential, and fail to name specifically what "actor" performs what action and in what order.

There are a few concepts that are essential if the writer of the procedure is to develop a more useful management procedure. These concepts include the systems cycle, the main line, the big show, the trigger, and the result.

Procedures should not include long lists of detailed steps followed by only one actor. The related task outline can serve here. Neither should a procedure list all the captions on a printed form. If the form's captions are so poor that they are not clear, revise the form. Do not list, in a procedure, where the eight copies of a form's set are to go. Do that on the form itself. In the procedure simply say, "Distributes all the required copies."

The chaos that we know as the document jungle will only be eliminated when:

1. Top executives take an interest in and know intimately all their own key documents. There are only 30 or 40 of them.

2. They assign a capable management documents developer to do the documents job.

Playscript, developed by the author decades ago, is suitable to use as a standard procedure in any type of organization, including those in business, financial, governmental, insurance, and military fields. Unfortunately, from our sampling, we find that people often "modify" *Playscript,* using a version that we developed, tested, and rejected many years ago. This is progressing "backwards." *Playscript,* in its pure form, is a powerful management tool, a real document to manage by.

Chapter 6

AUTHORITY TO APPROVE

A department manager calls a long-time employee into his office and says: "Starting Monday, Barbara, you'll be the supervisor of your section." That statement catapults Barbara into a new world . . . into the world of giving orders rather than taking them. She may wonder about her new job . . . but one question will stand out: "As a supervisor, what *responsibility* and *authority* do I have?"

Probably no one, not even her boss, will tell her. She may ask herself, for example: "If I am responsible for getting this work done, can I hire good people? Can I fire those subordinates who aren't doing well now?"

She'll probably find that she cannot hire and fire entirely on her own. Such personnel actions will probably require her boss's approval, as well as the approval of someone in the Personnel Department.

It is likely that Barbara's company does issue a chart on authorities. Most companies do not. Of course, Barbara's name is not now on that "authority to approve" chart. How does her manager get her name on? In the meantime she will need a copy of the current chart.

What authority must she exercise based on the *work* she does? Give orders? Approve certain forms and reports? EXAMPLE: As supervisor of the telephone room, Barbara does have the right to call the phone company and have them install a special control for the phone operators. No other supervisor can do that.

149

Her right to do so stems from her "work needs" authority. What authority does she have in common with other supervisors?

To get her name on the authority chart, Barbara's manager fills out and signs a form titled AUTHORITY REQUEST. Copies of the form go to a selected list of people, including the person who will revise and reissue the authority chart. Who are those people?

Over a period of time any such chart will need deletions as well as additions. People leave, they die, they move away, they transfer, they quit . . . or they are promoted to where their specialized work authorities are no longer needed.

A policy covering authority lays the foundation for the company's entire authority pattern. As we have said, a policy tells *what* to do but *not* how to do it. So Barbara's manager needs a *how-to* procedure, a step-by-step guide on how to put his newly appointed supervisor on the official authority chart.

A PLAYSCRIPT PROCEDURE

Subject: Securing Approval Authority for a Supervisor

Who	**Does What**
Department Manager	1. Requests that Personnel send a prenumbered copy of form CA-1141, AUTHORITY NOTICE.
	2. Fills out forms set, approves, then calls in the newly appointed supervisor.
	3. Provides new supervisor with one copy of the filled out CA-1141. Also provides a copy of POLICY 79 and the latest revision of Form 642, AUTHORITY PATTERN.
	4. Explain both (1) all supervisors' common supervisory authority and (2) the new supervisor's specific work-connected authority.

Who		**Does What**
New Supervisor	5.	Asks questions or requests any clarifications.
Department Manager	6.	Retrieves new supervisor's copy of Form CA-1141, pointing out that it requires further approval. Sends entire forms set to Personnel.
Assistant Personnel Manager	7.	Checks Form CA-1141 on the authority control log. Consults the applicable policy (No. 79).
	7a.	If any questions, contacts the requesting manager by phone.
	8.	Sets effective date.
	9.	Personally delivers the numbered master to the manager or to the department secretary.
Department Manager	10.	Checks the specific authorities on which the employee must have approval authority in order to carry on her (or his) work.
	11.	Secures specimen of new supervisor's signature.
	12.	Reviews authority extent and limits of authority with the new supervisor.
	13.	Signs and asks secretary to personally deliver Form CA-1141 to the Assistant Personnel Manager.
Assistant Personnel Manager	14.	Arranges for the reproduction of the required number of copies of Form 642, AUTHORITY PATTERN.
	15.	Controls all waste copies and the master by specifying reproduction on a "supervised" basis.

Who	Does What
Assistant Personnel Manager	16. Issues required number of copies of the revised Form 642, AUTHORITY PATTERN.
	17. Files one copy of Form 642, and two copies of CA-1141 in the current revision file.

1. WHAT IS AUTHORITY?

According to a scholar on the origin of words, the letters AU are derived from the French language and stand for *with the.* The letters THOR come to us from the mythical god of thunder, worshiped in the ancient world. Thus au-thor-ity carries a meaning of "with the power and the might." A person in authority is a person in command. An individual cited as an expert becomes an authority on a specific subject. The word authority is related to words such as *decision, power,* or *legal right.*

In a manufacturing company, the executive committee became disturbed by reports of numerous actions taken by men and women who did not have the authority to take such actions. The committee chairman, who was also the vice-president of administration, assigned a senior analyst to study the present authority-to-approve situation and to recommend how it could be made less confusing. In the study, she found that people did not distinguish the real meanings of terms related to the exercise of authority, such as:

1.	Approved	6.	Authorized
2.	Signed	7.	Ratified
3.	Endorsed	8.	Recommended
4.	Requested	9.	Confirmed
5.	Certified	10.	Read and Noted

The analyst studied the major "business forms" that carried authority to spend money or to do work. Who told the forms designer to call for approvals on certain forms? The analyst concentrated on the forms captions that implied that the person was exercising authority. One caption stated "Supervisor's signature." What did it mean? She also studied the major (big show) procedures. Some approval authority had been delegated in memos. The analyst contacted the company's forms design specialist. He said that he had never seen any type of management document that spelled out all the authority patterns. When asked why he would use "approval" or similar words on some forms, he said it was almost always because the previous versions of that form had carried such terms. Obviously no one had ever thought much about who had what authority.

The analyst discovered one memo, issued years before, by a controller who was no longer in the company. An excerpt from the memo looked like this:

Subject: APPROVALS ACCEPTABLE TO ACCOUNTING

Document	Source	Authority	Financial Limitations
Purchasing Requisition	Corporate Office or Plants	President	Unlimited
		Exec. Vice President	$75,000
		V.P. & Controller	$25,000
		V.P. & Secretary	$20,000
		V.P. & Treasurer	$20,000
		Plant Manager	$15,000
		Assist. Controller	$10,000
Invoice from Vendor or a Consultant	Corporate Office	President	Unlimited
		Exec. Vice President	$500,000
		Treas. Corp. Sec.	$200,000
		V.P. & Treasurer	$200,000
		V.P. & Controller	$100,000
		Assist. Controller	$ 50,000
	Departments	Manager	$ 25,000

The entire memo included a total of 11 "authorizing" forms and all were based on monetary approval limits.

A more useful pattern, in another company, was in a matrix form, a rectangular array of elements that included the types of authority and the individual (using people's names) who could exercise each authority. The arrangement resembled a multiplication table or a decision table.

People's names were listed in the vertical first column on the left. The authority types were listed across the top of the form, at a 45° angle.

When asked to comment on it, we recommended that the document carry work titles, such as vice-president, manager, manager of purchasing, supervisor of transportation, etc. We suggested that they not use individuals' names. Job titles reflect continuing functions so they are more "stable" than are the human assignments to those jobs.

2.   ADVICE OR AUTHORITY?

In a planned factory expansion, the project manager couldn't seem to wrap up the planning phases. He called meeting after meeting, yet had difficulty in securing approvals from supervisors and managers who would be involved in the expansion. His boss, the manufacturing vice-president, grew impatient with the delays and he called together all the people who had a part in the planning. He expected from 10 to 12 men and women but 67 people came!

Even under the vice-president's chairmanship the meeting was still inconclusive. So he asked, "Why do sixty-seven people have to approve?" In a few days his staff assistant verified that each of the 67 men and women did have a "stake" in the new factory addition.

Then the vice-president realized that his project manager had made no distinction between the *authority to approve* . . . and the function of *considering* the various work needs in the new plant.

EXAMPLES: The supervisor of Internal Transportation attended the meeting so that he could explain (for one thing) that the aisles must be wide enough so that his operators (on electric trucks) could swing around the corners with a train of two or three cars. The chief operator of the phone services was concerned about the arrangement of new connections with her present switchboard.

The vice-president concluded that his subordinates had used the word *approval* too loosely. In most instances the 67 people were *not* called upon to approve. Their roles were advisory.

They merely needed to contribute information on their special physical requirements. Only four of the 67 people should have had approval authority.

But the other 63 men and women thought they were expected to approve. As a by-product of his experience, the vice-president assigned his staff assistant a job, saying:

> Develop a pattern of authority that can guide our people. I want an on-its-toes organization that can move . . . can get action! We can't confuse the exercise of authority with other management functions. Develop such an authority pattern for this division. Coordinate it with the corporate people, then bring it in for my approval.

Like a policy or a procedure, delegation of authority requires a management decision. WHO must have the authority to approve WHAT? Decide. Then inform both (1) the people who are to exercise the delegated authority and (2) the people who are on the *receiving* end of the authority flow.

Decisions on approvals, however, can rarely be unilateral. The people who will be affected need to be heard. Those who will exercise authority must listen to people whose role is advisory. That is the vital, but sensible step that we call "coordination."

3.   THE THREE FACETS OF AUTHORITY

Are there different types of authority? We can identify at least three major facets of authority:

1.   Authority *common* to a position or rank, such as that of all supervisors
2.   *Work needs* authority
3.   *Work flow* authority

There are others. An example of *common* authority would be that "all supervisors are authorized to approve a stockroom requisition." An example of *work needs* authority would be that "only engineering supervisors are authorized to approve the release of a new or revised engineering drawing." The *work flow* authority stems from a management system and is stated in the related procedure. EXAMPLE: A customer's purchase order will set off a flow of work authority for dozens of people as soon as the order is released into the order processing system.

Authority contained in the work flow is not always visible but it does exist. It consists of a chain of authorities, one linked to the next. Let's illustrate this type of authority with an example of how hard the flow authority is to "breach." An assistant to the research vice-president in a manufacturing company, as one of his duties, initiated a specialized research project. Needing some machine work done on a special jig (a positioning tool), he secured a copy of the factory's tool fabrication order, filled it out, signed it in the space with the caption "authorized by," and sent it to the machine shop.

The machine shop supervisor declined to honor that tool fabrication order since it did not come through the release system. So he referred it to the manufacturing control manager. This man called personally on the requester and pointed out that all work authority must flow through the production *systems channel.* He explained that otherwise anyone could authorize work to be done.

In the conversation the control manager traced the chain of authority (to do work) back to a customer's purchase order. The assistant to the vice-president, to get his special work done, needed to request that his superior, the vice-president, first approve a special form . . . AUTHORITY FOR INTERNAL EXPENDITURE.

It is easy to forget that there are two "actors" in any authority transfer . . . the *sender* and the *receiver.* In the previous example, the supervisor of the machine shop was the receiver.

The first actor is the person who has the right to approve something. The other actor is the receiver of that approved request. The receiver may ask: "Should I or should I not honor this request?" *Another example*: An employee (who worked in the materiel department) came to a production stockroom window and presented a requisition for a selected number of stock items. The employee's supervisor (a buyer) had signed the form.

The stockroom clerk had never provided these items to someone outside of her own production department. Should she provide the items, even with the signature of the employee's supervisor? How could she know whether that supervisor (in a different department) had the authority to approve a requisition for an item that normally is only drawn out by people who work in the production department?

 It is just as important to inform people who are on the receiving end of authority documents as it is to let those know who *have* the authority that they do have it.

Receivers of authority can be so informed, of course, by receiving a copy of whatever authority document you distribute. People who are frequently on the receiving end of an authority transfer include:

1.	Timekeepers	7.	Shipping clerks
2.	Data processors	8.	Repairmen
3.	Cashiers	9.	Word processors
4.	Receptionists	10.	Employment interviewers
5.	Warehousemen	11.	Pay masters
6.	Security guards	12.	Tool crib clerks

Once you've identified these receivers of authority they'll need a copy of your authority pattern document. However, in some critical situations, the person expected to accept the authority may require a specimen signature, such as is usually required in banking transactions.

More examples of common authorities to approve include: the transfer of an employee, a wage change, a package pass, vacation pay, a leave of absence, procuring work station supplies.

The more limited work-needs approval authority includes these examples:

Release of a manufacturing order, contract for consulting services, approving a medical claim, change of insurance coverage, initiating a product research project, purchase of new data processing hardware, the sale of surplus equipment, the purchase of special tooling, borrowing money.

One person's authority to approve can be derived from various sources. The *two* major sources are (1) the common authorities that come with the title, such as that of supervisor, foreman, or manager (ranks) and (2) the authority that the person requires due to his or her responsibility for a specific segment of the organization's work. For example, all supervisors may have the authority to approve a package pass for any one of that supervisor's subordinates. But do they have the right to O.K. a package pass for an employee who does not work *for them*? Do they have the authority to permit a loaded truck to leave the premises? A *work needs* approval will apply. Probably only the security supervisor has the right to approve the passage of a loaded truck out the security gate.

Another source of approval authority is that derived from a previously approved plan. EXAMPLE: Once a supervisor's budget has been approved by higher authorities, it conveys to that supervisor authority which he or she can exercise to spend money and thus to accomplish work. Since the budget has already been approved by higher authority, the supervisor has a *derived* authority, derived from the original approval of the budget plan. Further higher approval is not required. So types of authority can be summarized as:

1. *Positional.* Example: Supervisor.

2. *Job Related.* Example: A buyer in purchasing.

3. *Work Requirements.* Example: Maintenance requires cleaning materials.

4. *Procedural.* Derived from a systems plan.

5. *Derived* from a previous management approval such as a budget plan.

4. DOCUMENTING AUTHORITY

Naturally before recommending any new documents on approval authority, you'll find out what your organization has now. Make a quick survey.

Start with accounting. Financial people must have a knowledge of who can approve specific financial commitments, so they are likely to have some documentation. Somewhere in the accounting functional areas, you will find a list of approvals that are being accepted for financial expenditures.

Start with this financial authority in whatever form you may find it.

1. Probe the present "authority" situation.

   A. Talk to about six supervisors from entirely different functions about their *common* authority.

   B. Interview six *work specialist* supervisors (such as those in sales, inventory, production, or security).

   C. Study at least 10 of the major *forms*, looking for signature or approval spaces.

   D. Look for work flow authority. Read the 10 or 12 major procedures (those reflecting the "big show" systems). Spot and note each approval action called for.

   E. Gather any and all directives, policies, or memos on the subject of "authority."

2. Develop a list of *common authorities* that all supervisors exercise.

3. Prepare a work needs list of authorities. This will be unique to each work specialty area.

4. Arrange all of these in matrix chart form:

   A. Secure tentative approval from a top executive.

   B. Issue the chart as a "proposed" pattern. Distribute it widely. Invite suggestions and comments. Allow 15 days for comments to reach you.

5. Based on the information gathered and submitted finalize the matrix chart on authority. Secure final top-management approval (ask the president to sign the master copy).

6. Issue the authority chart for inclusion in a manual that goes to every member of management (this could be the *management* manual, the *systems* manual or the *corporate* manual).

7. Don't overlook the *receivers* of authority. Develop a list of these people. Ask the men and women, who do approve, who the people are who *respond* to their approvals. Provide extra copies for non-manual holders, but who act based on approvals (security people, stockroom clerks, buyers, accountants).

8. Supplement the chart with a policy statement covering the subject of "authority to approve" and have it signed by the chief executive officer.

9. Invite people to continue to make suggestions on what authority is or is not needed.

10. Set up a short-cycle system for changing the authority pattern for an individual. Write the procedure that reflects that system. Design and get approval on a printed form that people can use to initiate the change.

11. Be prepared to revise the chart or pattern frequently in the first four or five months . . . until the authority patterns "settle down."

A statement spelling out the decisions on *common authority* can be issued on a policy bulletin approved either by the president, the controller, or the vice-president of personnel (human resources). Our preference is the president.

A matrix chart may not be enough. Do consider the "big show" printed forms since they are major carriers of authority. Confer with your forms design people. Ask them to supply a sample of each form that calls for a signature, initial, or has a space for someone to sign. Frequently men and women who are not supervisors will sign. A receiving dock clerk is one example.

There are probably several hundred printed forms in your organization that carry authority (and somebody's approval for something). Here is a list of a few such forms:

Request for Check	Expense Reimbursement
Stop Order	Claim
Request for Auto	Request for Consulting Services
Travel Authority	Request for Cash Advance
Employee Transfer	Inter-Plant Material Transfer
Visitor's Pass	Request for Repairs
Shipping Order	Employee Rate Change

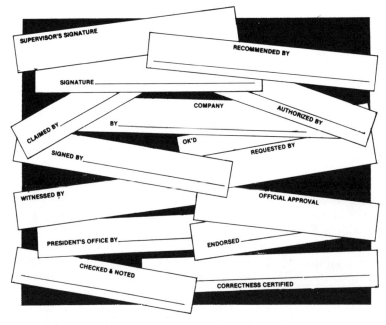

What do all the signature spaces mean? Approval? Recommendation? Request? How does the signer know that he (or she) has the authority to sign?

How to distribute the authority patterns can pose a problem. Who needs a copy of the matrix bulletin on authority? It is likely to be a document of several pages. Do run the information on the front and back of each sheet of paper.

One company puts out an in-plant and office directory with "inside" (extension) phone numbers. Management issues the directory every six months and codes the degree of authority for approvals, using asterisks or stars opposite the individual's name in the directory, like this:

	Extension
Sarah Roberts Allison**	2337
John F. Anderson*	6839
T. J. Axelson	4611

Ms. Allison's authority is coded by two asterisks, indicating that she is a department head. Mr. Anderson's single asterisk indicates that he has the common authority of a foreman. T. J. Axelson has no approval authority. Of course, only common authority can be shown in such a directory. The code, with from one to three stars or with from one to three asterisks, is explained in the front of the directory.

In the exercise of authority to approve, many questions can arise. If a supervisor signs an employee's attendance report, is this an approval to pay? Or is it verification of the employee's attendance? If the employee is working out of the plant (perhaps also out of the city), who approves his or her daily time sheet or time card? Is an imprint of the time clock enough to provide authority for the paymaster to pay the employee?

Without specific guidance on such approval actions, individuals tend toward a timidity that does not make for snappy action at the operational level.

They try to avoid "getting into trouble." Men and women who DO HAVE sufficient guidance, will know the extent and the limits of their authority. Then they can move swiftly to execute the work for which they are responsible.

If the authority to approve is not documented and is not communicated clearly, the door can be open to not only mistakes, but to fraud, misappropriation, and plain thievery.

Today white collar crime is rampant. The computer's portion of a management system provides an "open door" for knowledgeable thieves. Electronic codes can be broken, and the thievery can take place via a public pay phone. Then authority patterns that surround the company's vital data base (by which the entire data operation runs) must be carefully thought out, protected, and monitored.

Special authority to approve rests on work requirements. Consider the supervisor of the scrap and salvage section. He will require specific authority to approve. He will have the authority to approve passage out of the plant area of a loaded truck. The supervisor over another activity, for example, may not exercise such authority.

5. TO GET SNAPPY ACTION . . .

One of the reasons it can take two or three months to get a decision from a government bureaucracy (for a decision that a capable person could make in five minutes) is that too many transactions must go up the chain of command. Of course slow-moving bureaucracy is everywhere, not just in government. Big corporations are equally as ponderous.

If men and women in any (business or government) supervisory or management rank know exactly what they are responsible for, and exactly what they have the authority for approving or for doing, wouldn't the organization be able to move more swiftly . . . and get snappier results?

We do want people in the action fields to make swift decisions. But such decisions must be *in harmony* with management's directions and help in the process of moving toward the organization's goals!

Without a clear knowledge of people's specific authorities, a form of organizational paralysis sets in.

Authority to approve enlarges as you go up the chain of command . . . up the organization's hierarchy. A maintenance supervisor could not approve the purchase of a new building. However, the company president could.

6. SUMMARY

The distribution of authority to approve requires a myriad of decisions. Start that distribution by listing and making clear, in one document, the authority of position by titles . . . the common authority. EXAMPLES: All supervisors have *these* authorities. All managers have *these*. All department heads have *these*. If your people-title structure is a jumble, clean that up first. Otherwise it will be difficult to assign common authority.

Special authority goes with the work to be done. The sales manager can approve selling expense. The buying manager cannot.

There is only one reason for giving people authority to approve and that is so that they can carry on their work. Then the organization can get its required results without losing control over its resources and assets.

The ideal is that each supervisor and each manager will have exactly the amount of authority that he or she needs to carry out the assigned responsibility. No more. No less.

Authority goes down the chain of command by delegation. Much depends upon the good judgment of the manager who delegates his or her authority to a supervisor to see that the authority delegated is just enough but not too much.

When people do exercise their authority to approve, they will also be spending the organization's resources of (1) time, (2) materials, (3) services, or (4) money.

Chapter 7

TITLES THAT COMMUNICATE

What does the word "manager" mean? How about "supervisor?" Is it a synonym for manager?

If the subject of management documents is to be discussed fruitfully, two people must come to at least a reasonable agreement on the meanings of the terms they use. Without such common meanings, the area of management communication will remain a jungle.

Someone has said that two people can only converse (communicate) in a productive manner when they can name the specific items they're talking about.

Your organization may be different and all management positional terms may be well-defined. If so, yours is a unique situation. From my own observations I'd say that most management terms are not universally defined. So we should consider, at least briefly, what the commonly used titles should mean and how they should be defined. Titles of concern include:

1. Titles for people
2. Titles of the organization's segments
3. Titles of documents to manage by

1. TITLES FOR PEOPLE

If you say, "Let's send a copy of this policy to all supervisors," will each supervisor really need *that* policy? The answer will depend upon how well you've defined the job covered by the title of *supervisor*. In one large company where the management wanted to achieve uniform meanings of titles, the word *supervisor* meant a man or woman who *supervised* the workers. (They were the sergeants or the lieutenants on the "firing line.") No one could use the term supervisor who did not oversee and take the responsibility for the work of five or more persons.

The term *manager* was reserved to mean a person who supervised supervisors. In one hierarchical stack, there were as many as 11 levels between the worker and the chairman of the board. They needed a term to describe a position between that of manager and of supervisor. So they used the term *general* supervisor. This term meant that the individual was responsible for directing two or more supervisors.

They also had to go the other way, downward a notch, particularly when there were several work shifts. So one term used was *assistant* supervisor. The term "assistant" was also used for subordinate supervisors when it was obvious that the span of control was beyond one person.

EXAMPLE: In one office department a supervisor was helped by two assistant supervisors because there were 47 workers. However, the role of each person was carefully spelled out. The supervisor himself took on direct responsibility for the output of 11 people.

The hierarchy in this rather large company was a "chain of command," lowest rank to the highest, like this:

1.	Chairman of the Board	7.	Department Head
2.	President	8.	Manager
3.	Executive Vice-President	9.	General Supervisor
4.	Senior Vice-President	10.	Supervisor
5.	Vice-President	11.	Assistant Supervisor
6.	Assistant Vice-President	12.	Worker

Time-honored titles such as *controller* and *purchasing agent* were not abolished but were defined as equivalents. The controller was a vice-president (of finance) and the purchasing agent was a department head (of purchasing). He reported to the vice-president of Materiel, as did the warehouse and stockroom managers.

Our entire focus in this book has been on the people and the work that they do. We also ask: "How well are the individual efforts fitted into the various teamwork patterns?" To paraphrase a great British consultant:

The effectiveness of an organization is coming to depend less and less on the efficiency of individual effort (as important as that is) and to become more and more dependent upon the precision with which those individual efforts are joined.   — *Lyndall Urwick*

American and Canadian managers are certainly concerned with our serious decline in productivity. The factors that contribute to such a decline could include government regulatory interference, noncooperation from labor leaders, the tax structure that diverts capital improvement funds into excessive "welfare" distribution, etc. But all the sad stories come back to roost on management. Just how precisely do your various managers coordinate the hundreds of individual efforts into a coordinated whole? The answer could be: *Not nearly as well as they could.*

Quality management documents can be useful tools for securing a higher degree of coordination, making them truly documents to manage by.

Uniformity of titles of people within the management cadre is important to a clear understanding of the *work* that they do. Giving out titles like "manager" to someone who doesn't manage may seem like a fun game. A bit laughable perhaps. But such playing does not help clear up the internal communications muddle.

From your current organization charts, directories, and other documents in your organization, gather and list all the titles. Package them by rank. You may have a six-level hierarchy. If so at what level does each title reside?

We will not attempt that task here but we will summarize the approaches we've found practical in bringing definite meaning to each title.

First define what a supervisor is. The supervisor is the first link between the worker and management and exercises discipline over the workers. To the worker the supervisor *is* management. The supervisor guides subordinates and shares with his or her experienced employees any new working techniques. Finally, the supervisor sees that the employees who are to do the work actually do it and that they do it well.

At the other end of the chain of command, the chief executive officer (CEO) is responsible for the success of all operations. This man or woman is expected to be a generalist, not a specialist. Yet that person had to climb to the position of "general executive" through some field of specialized work . . . perhaps sales, engineering, or law. The CEO could be the president or he or she could be the executive vice-president.

Right under the chief of operations will be a series of top chief *work specialists* . . . usually vice-presidents. One will be the vice-president of marketing . . . another of accounting . . . another of production . . . another of personnel . . . and still another of materiel.

2. DEVELOPING A GOOD TITLE FOR PEOPLE

How do you select a meaningful title for an individual position? Do it this way:

1. Select a word that describes a general field of work, such as sales, control, finance, or transportation.

2. Select a second word that describes a specialty within that field . . . *national* sales or *air* transportation.

3. Select another word that describes the position or rank. It could be manager, supervisor, chief, or department head.

Can a man's or woman's position be described with one word? Not often. Referring to airplanes, the term *pilot* does mean an individual who can fly an airplane. Now if you add the term *test* to the term *pilot*, you get *test pilot*. Now you have a specific title and it tells people that the individual is a pilot (can fly an airplane) and that he also tests airplanes.

Now if he supervises the work of say a dozen test pilots, he becomes the *chief test pilot*. Now the title would tell any reader that:

1. The person is a flyer . . . a *pilot*.
2. That he is a specific type of pilot, one who *tests* aircraft.
3. That he is an executive . . . a *chief* over this specialized work.

Would you now feel that the position title is one that carries a rather precise meaning?

Consider another work title, that of *buyer*. We know that this person will be buying articles, items, materials, or services for the organization. By adding the two words *electric products* to the title we get *electric products buyer*. This will tell a reader a great deal about that buyer . . . that his work consists of buying electric products.

Do not take it for granted that the job descriptions provided by the wage and salary people describe the work as well as you would want it to be described. Personnel titles are used to rate jobs as to salary and other categories and such titles are backed up with a complete job description. At least these can be a start toward a title suitable for use in connection with management documents.

Your title for a position is likely to be limited to two or three words. Do not be bashful about suggesting that Personnel change the position title if it doesn't now seem to describe the work adequately.

Let's consider another time-honored title . . . chief. What does the word *chief* mean? Frequently the chief engineer is the top executive over the specialized work known as engineering.

You've seen titles reflecting specialized work such as . . . *chief* of quality control, *chief* of traffic, *chief* of research and development, or *chief* of auditing.

There can be a chief telephone operator, a person in an executive position who is responsible for the performance of the phone and transmission machine operators. There can be a chief teller in a bank . . . or chief dispatcher for rail or taxi activi-

ties. And there can be a chief inspector in a quality control operation.

At the working level some people serve both as workers and as
bosses. Sometimes we refer to them as "straw bosses."

Titles can be enlarged or reduced. Two modifying terms are
widely used . . . *general* and *assistant*. Take the term *sales manager*,
then add the word *general* and you get *general sales manager*. You
know that this title represents a position that is at least one step
higher than that of *sales manager*.

The title of sales manager can also be reduced a notch by using the term *assistant*, giving you *assistant sales manager*. This tells
the story of this person's position. Anyone seeing this title would
recognize that the individual is in a management position, but
that the position is one notch below that of a full-blown sales
manager.

Other enlarging or reducing titles include: senior, junior, act-
ing, lead, petty, junior, and trainee.

President is a top management title. But we don't call his immediate subordinates assistant presidents. We call them vice-presidents. Usually a vice-president will head up a work specialty.
One vice-president heads up finance, another production, and
another sales. Their departments are separate *compartments*, enclosing special work skills. It is the president's job (the only generalist) to see that these chief work specialists and their people
cooperate with each other. But the president can't do it all personally. He needs and uses help from his numerous *management
systems* and he uses management documents to make his will
known to all.

3.   TITLES FOR ORGANIZATIONAL SUB-UNITS

What is a department? A plant? A section or a group? Is a department the major sub-unit? If your company is a conglomer-
ate, what are the divisions called? Subsidiaries?

Do you now have a set of standard names that apply to the
sub-units? If you can't find such standards, talk to the long-
range planner and to the head of Personnel. They have undoubtedly given the subject considerable thought.

In your basic organization chart, you do not include the term
"department." That is, in the block depicting the marketing

function the term is simply MARKETING, a term representing work. Departments are usually the major sub-units, including the "big show" activities and the major supporting units. Sometimes there are two big shows. Production and marketing in a company may receive major support from personnel, finance, administration, and materiel.

To describe a sub-unit usually requires two words. The first word represents the work for which the unit is responsible, and the second word tells what kind of a unit it is:

Engineering Department
Design Section
Drafting Group

Here is one company's list of functions for its sub-units, along with related people titles. They may serve as idea starters when you are considering names for your sub-units:

CORPORATE   Chairman of the Board
                                   President
                                   Secretary
                                   Treasurer

Sub-units	Titles for Executives
Office of the President	Executive Vice-President Chief Executive Officer Senior Vice-President
Subsidiary	Subsidiary President Vice-President Plant Manager
Division	Vice-President Division Manager Engineering Chief Controller Purchasing Agent
Department	Department Head Chief (Engineering functions) Director Cashier Administrator Manager

Sub-units	Titles for Executives
Section	Manager (Nonengineering functions) Chief of Quality Control Superintendent (Production or Maintenance functions)
Subsection	General Supervisor (General Foreman in a Factory) Assistant Superintendent Captain (in Plant Security) Fire Chief Medical Director Safety Engineer

Group — Office or Shop	Supervisor (Responsible for office
	    functions)
	Foreman (Responsible for factory
	    functions)

Gang, Crew or Shift	Group leader Leadman or leadwoman Head foreman or head forelady Team leader

The following is an example of an industrial organization's "departmental" line up. It also includes the four-digit numbering plan that worked out quite well in practice. The numbers were significant (each group did represent one work specialty) but at the same time permitted flexibility as changes took place. The total employment was 17,500.

Organization Number	Function
100	CORPORATE OFFICE
101	Legal Counsel
102	Stockholder Relations
103	Planning, Short & Long
104	Management Audits
105	Organizational Analysis
106	Management Documentation
107	Staff Projects
108	Community Relations

Organization Number	*Function*
2000	MARKETING
2001	Sales
2002	Advertising
2003	Sales Promotion
2004	Estimating
2005	Order Processing
2006	Market Forecasting
2007	Pricing (shared with Cost Accounting)
2008	Market Research
2009	Sales Offices
2010	Customer Field Services
2011	Publicity
2012	Liaison with Engineering
3000	ENGINEERING
3001	Design
3002	Drafting
3003	Blueprints & Whiteprints
3004	Print Release & Control
3005	Research & Development
3006	Product & Design Testing
3007	Administrative Engineering
3008	Liaison Engineering
3009	Field Engineering
3010	Model Shop
3011	Quality Control
3012	Experimental Research
3013	Operations Research
4000	MANUFACTURING
4001	Fabrication
4002	Assembly
4003	Experimental Manufacturing
4004	Tool Manufacturing
4005	Machine Shop
4006	Sheet Metal Shop

Organization Number	*Function*
4007	Chemical Processing
4008	Process Control
4009	Plant Maintenance
4010	Plant Engineering
4011	Industrial Engineering
4012	Equipment & Property Control
4013	Make or Buy Group
4014	Methods
4015	Night Shift
5000	PRODUCTION CONTROL
5001	Manufacturing Control
5002	Outside Manufacturing
5003	Perishable Tools
5004	Tool Control
5005	On-line Stores
5006	Scheduling
5007	Internal Transportation
6000	MATERIEL

6001	Buying
	   a. Raw materials
	   b. Purchased parts
	   c. Special components
	   d. Purchasing services

6002	Shipping
6003	Salvage & Disposal
6004	Stores & Warehouses
6005	Material Control
6006	Materials Research
6007	Inventory Records
6008	Trucks
7000	TOOLING
7001	Tool Design
7002	Tool Liaison
7003	Tool Fabrication

Organization Number	*Function*
7004	Tool Testing
7005	Tool Proving
7006	Tool Control
7007	Tool Repair or Revision
8000	ACCOUNTING & FINANCE
8001	Accounts Payable
8002	Accounts Receivable
8003	Payroll
8004	General Accounting
8005	Billing
8006	Credits & Collections
8007	Budgets
8008	Cost Accounting & Pricing
8009	Timekeeping
8010	Property Accounting
8011	Taxes
8012	Audits
9000	ADMINISTRATIVE SERVICES
9001	External Transportation
9002	Manuals
9003	Word Processing
9004	Suggestion Awards Program
9005	U.S. Mail
9006	Internal Mail
9007	Records Management
9008	In-house Printing
9009	Copiers
9010	Office Equipment
9011	Receiving
9012	Travel & Reservations
9013	Data Processing — Distributed
9014	D P Training
9015	Mail Equipment Development
9016	Motor Pool

176

DOCUMENTS TO MANAGE BY

Organization Number	Function
9500	INDUSTRIAL RELATIONS
9501	Plant & Office Security
9502	Employment
9503	Labor Relations
9504	Medical & Health
9505	Employee Services
9506	Training
9507	Wage & Salary
9508	Union Negotiation
9509	Credit Union
9510	Government Liaison
1000	MANAGEMENT INFORMATION
1001	Systems Analysis
1002	Programming
1003	Data Entry (key punch)
1004	Computer Operations — Central
1005	Data Library
1006	Data Security
1007	Technical & Equipment Research
1008	Procedures
1009	Forms Control
1010	Software Research
1011	Reports Control
1012	Testing
1013	Documentation

4. DOCUMENT TITLES

REMINDER: You cannot think, speak, teach, or write about anything accurately until you *name* it . . . specifically. You can't even discuss "it."

To make better management communication possible, call each document what it is. Forget your present and past-document titles. Most of them do not tell what the document is, nor do they enlighten the reader on their purposes. Vagueness in the document title detracts from the clearness of the message that it carries. Most old, even familiar, document titles have failed so miserably that there is only one place for them . . . in the trash barrel.

Do you want people to understand that you *are* making a statement of policy? Then put the word P O L I C Y at the top of the document. If it is another kind of document, such as a statement of work, put that at the top: STATEMENT OF WORK. An organization chart is more obvious, but do use that title: ORGANIZATION CHART. The same advice is true with procedures or approval authority documents. Call them what they *are*!

When it comes to naming the procedure, don't continue to go along with standard instructions, standard procedures, divisional instructions, manual of procedures, standard practice instructions, standard practice procedures, controller's procedures, methods bulletins, standard practice memos . . . and all such bulletins with vague titles. How much simpler if you have a document that looks like this:

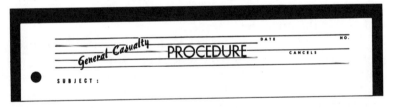

Repeated experience shows that even after people name documents, they add all types of "busy-business" at the top of the document. Such details make the document look dull, legalistic, and even foreboding. Most of those items are not necessary.

After the word that tells the reader what the document is . . . procedure, policy, statement of work, or whatever . . . all else that the reader needs is the *date* and the *number* of the document. If it's a revision or replacement, then do add the date and the number of the document that this one cancels. What else can be needed? Your executives may want the caption "effective date" instead of just "date." Fine.

Keep the heading clean and sharp. Shout out from the housetops exactly what the document is. No pussyfooting.

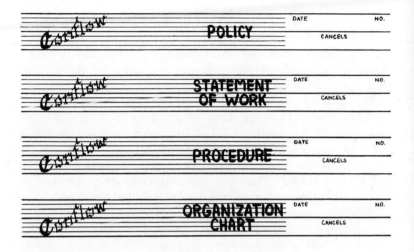

With precise, meaningful titles your management documents will be well started. Your next item, of course, near the top of the page, is the *Subject.* Place it in the upper left corner.

A few other additions can be used without detracting from the appearance of the bulletin. How about the company insignia? Maybe in the upper left corner?

If each bulletin needs an approval signature, provide space for it, usually at the end. One other item: If the "message" will apply only temporarily, add a termination date.

So you will have a simple self-explanatory title for each document. Then, if you write the document clearly and you distribute it to all people who need it, you've developed a set of quality documents . . . documents to manage by.

But, lest someone forgets, documents are only tools. Remind the tool *users* of that fact. Don't ever let them think that a set of good documents can do what only men and women can do.

Chapter 8

COMMON ERRORS IN
MANAGEMENT DOCUMENTATION
and How to Avoid Them

In any new program it is easy to do things wrong. And if errors are compounded the whole program can collapse. This is true of a management documents program, particularly policies and statements of work.

In my first experience in the development of management documents the chairman (a member of the big corporation's board of directors) made a number of errors. I was one of seven people on the man's "management task force", and I made my share of mistakes, too. Of course we didn't recognize them as errors until after we had completed our work.

During my second experience with management analysis and the resulting documents (this time I served as the project leader), our small team tried to avoid most of those earlier errors. Of course, we made a few new errors. The following is an attempt to warn both company executives and their document developers about certain common errors . . . so that all of you can avoid them. Most of these errors can occur in the statement of work portion of the documents program.

ERROR 1. NOT PREPARING PEOPLE FOR THE DOCUMENTS PROGRAM

Request the chief executive to explain the program in one of his staff meetings. Send out a notice as a letter from the highest executive (the chief executive officer) telling why the company needs these documents. The greatest danger here lies in the statements of work. Caution the department people that they are not to write the statements until the detailed guidance has been made available. Mention that they will be working with the developer as co-author.

ERROR 2. NOT PROVIDING GUIDANCE

This is an amateur's way. The attitude is, "Don't bother with guidance. Just tell the executives to write up what their departments do." Try that and you will be sorry. You will be snowed under the heaps of glorious statements, mostly "whitewash." You could be a year or more untangling the mess.

When you dig in to correct all the "snow jobs," you will create *resentment* and *resistance* where none should exist. The feelings of the executives will be hurt. A high-level manager may think, "Who is she (or he) to be revising what I wrote. She doesn't know our work."

Heed the voice of experience, some of it bitter. Do it the right way. Prepare and provide written guidance.

Each organizational unit, often in the person of the supervisor or manager, has a natural tendency to say, "Aren't we wonderful!" If you permit it, you will get an unrealistic rendering of "hearts and flowers." "Our people work so hard." "They accomplish so much." "We are so short-handed. We've just got to have more people." If a reader believed what they wrote, he would think that the people in that *single unit* really were the entire company.

Without guidance, instead of useful statements, you can receive much puffery, bull, and exaggeration.

ERROR 3. NOT MAKING IT CLEAR THAT THE WRITING WILL BE REVISED

Developing statements of work is a co-author proposition. Most managers are not good writers. But they do (or should) know what their people are doing. So each manager will be a co-author with the document developer. Managers and supervisors write the first drafts, adhering to the provided guidance.

Avoid being trapped in an avalance of papers and words. Provide writing guides. Speak of these as insuring a "corporate language."

When the chief executive issues his notice that introduces the program, make it clear that the developer will revise the statements, but will also recheck the revision with the originator.

ERROR 4.   NOT STARTING WITH ONE DEPARTMENT

If you put out the "go" signal to all departments at once, you could be inundated with drafts. Set priorities.

Do not put the "go" notice out to all departments at once. First select your one "big show" department. Send the notice out to all of that department's managers and supervisors. But before you do so, contact the department manager personally. He or she will write the overall statement of work for the entire department. This will become the summary that goes at the top of the statement. In this manner the developer can "feel his way" into the project.

ERROR 5. NOT ASKING FOR STAFF SIZE

Each sentence in the statement of work represents a specific type of work. How many people does it take to do it? Top executives will want to know. Gather that information with the drafts. When the statement is ready to publish and distribute, do not show staff size, but do add the staff size figures for the chief executive officer on his or her published copy. Show the staff size in parentheses, like this:

Publishes a monthly house organ for all employees. (7)

ERROR 6. NOT ASKING THE PRESIDENT TO BE BLUNT

Suggest that he say this right out:

We don't want any wordy fluff in this program. State simply what each group of people do. We are serious about it. We want to know what people are doing so we can make all of our functions visible to everyone, including yourself. Each statement will be reviewed critically. Now, you'll get a set of guides. Mr. or Miss (the developer) will bring them to you personally. Please take 15 minutes to review these guides. You will write the first drafts, either personally or have a staff person do it. Mr. or Miss (the developer) will work over the draft so that all writing will be uniform. The revision will then be returned to you to check for accuracy. Before completion the drafts may take several revisions.

The CEO doesn't say whether he will review it or if you will. Leave it that way.

ERROR 7.   PERMITTING ERUDITE LANGUAGE

Documents to manage by are not scholarly treatises. Write your statements of work in hard-hitting language that everybody can understand. Use your list of work words to prevent "erudition." Write in simple English. Do include words from your firm's *universally understood* shop language. Almost everybody in an oil company, for example, knows what *lease* means, or what a *core sample* is, or the meaning of the word *seismograph*. Just be sure that the added "shop talk" words *are* known throughout your corporation. Avoid "dark writing." It is that heavy stuff you find in so many management bulletins, books, and "professional" journals. Dark writing sheds little light on the subject. It is the type of writing that (while it may be grammatically O.K.) does not carry a management message. Dark writing also includes the unrevised kind of writing that is so easy for the writer to babble out, but very hard for the reader to read and to understand. Dark writing includes words and initials that your readers do not know. It often reflects the writer's anxiety and desire to impress other people.

ERROR 8.   INCLUDING COMMON DUTIES

If everybody listed every common duty, the normal one- or two-page statement of work could expand to five or six pages. If a duty is common to all, why state it dozens of times? Make it clear what common duties are. Tell the writers they're not wanted. Give examples of common duties.

ERROR 9.   PERMITTING A STATEMENT ON
PHANTOM WORK

The voice of experience in management documentation warns that some statement sentences will come through that:

1. Are what somebody in that department *should* be doing but nobody is.

2. Consist of "dream work." This is an activity that someone in the department *hopes* to be doing . . . some day.

Permit no statement of phantom work. The staff size figures will help you spot such ethereal "work." If there are no people doing that work, ask why. Also ask:

1. How long has this activity been pursued?
2. What are the results to date?
3. How much space is required (in square feet)?
4. What supplies or equipment are used?
5. What is the annual budget?

ERROR 10. NOT MAINTAINING THE STATEMENTS

A management document that is obsolete is of no value. Activities change, shift, end, or start. If your financial reports were six months old when your executives received them, would they be good decision tools? Of course not. Your statements of work won't be revised monthly but do set a regular time for their review and reissue. Also decide *who* will do it. *How* will that person know about a change in the work assignments?

Review all management documents quarterly. Pick up any normal changes and reissue the document. If a major change takes place, reissue the revised documents immediately. Obsolete documents have no value to members of management.

Documents Check List

OC = Organization Chart   SW = Statement of Work   PO = Policy
AA = Authority to Approve   PR = Procedures

Type	No.	Subject	Latest Date	Check if Short
PO	17	Use of company stationery	Mar. 11, 1981	
PO	36	Badge control	Feb. 3, 1982	
PO	76	Part time work	June 1, 1981	
OC	11	Quality control	May 15, 1982	
PR	142	Welding certification	July 5, 1982	
PR	11	Interoffice transfers	Feb. 16, 1982	
SW	7	Safety committee	Apr. 12, 1982	
AA	4	1982 Revision of authority to approve	July 16, 1982	
OC	3	Human resources	Nov. 3, 1981	
PO	82	Conflicts of interest	Oct. 30, 1981	
PR	241	Expense reimbursement	Mar. 6, 1982	
PR	103	Securing a company auto	Feb. 10, 1981	
PO	19	Restocking customer's returns	Sept. 18, 1980	
OC	2	Marketing	Aug. 8, 1981	

For Manual	Mail Station	Dept.
123	118	Human Resources

Check in right column if short. Return as a request to
Manuals Section, Mail Station 147

Periodically issue a purge (check list) for all documents and send it to each manual holder. The holder can use the same form as a requisition for missing documents. Then use it again as a covering "packing slip" to mail the documents to the manual holder.

Chapter 9

A DEVELOPER FOR MANAGEMENT
DOCUMENTS

Good documents to manage by don't just happen. If your company is unique and is already using a well-thought-out series of such documents, there must be a capable document developer somewhere in the background.

However, since only about one company in 50 (whether a large or a small organization) enjoys quality documents, chances are you don't have such a person. "That which is everybody's business is nobody's business." The consequence is a melange of documents, maybe most of them in memo form. It all adds up to documentary chaos ... a "normal" situation in both business and in government.

If you want effective management documents, appoint a man or woman who can do the job. *Be careful.* Don't appoint someone just because he is surplus and you don't know what else to do with him until his retirement. And do *not* appoint a clerk. Either way you'll never get the job done.

Do appoint a potential MANAGEMENT DOCUMENTS OFFICER. The title could be "administrative assistant" for the first year or two, until the developer wins his or her "wings." Some of the characteristics to look for in a candidate for this work (nobody will have all of them) include:

1. Reasonable intelligence.

2. Well-rounded education, probably a college graduate (but not overeducated).

3. Acceptable in appearance to most people (no weirdos).

4. Has at least four years of comprehensive business experience.

5. Can write *clearly* (a stenographer can correct the spelling).

6. Can talk plainly to people, singly or in groups.

7. A demonstrated analytical flair.

8. Self-starter . . . a project manager type . . . can push others to make them move, yet without arousing resentment.

9. Stable. Not a job jumper. (Check the record.)

10. Understands most business (or government) practices.

11. Positive attitude.

12. Knows most or all the facets of *your* business.

13. Understands completed staff work (shouldn't require over three hours a month of the big boss's time).

14. Able to distinguish between "big show" activities and minor support functions.

15. Without a doubt can in two years be worth 50 percent of a vice-president's salary.

16. Has a strong interest in such management matters as the span of control, delegation, or reports control.

17. Definitely not limited to technical knowledge such as programming, but does understand how to use a management tool such as the computer.

18. Is loyal to the firm, to its objectives and goals, and to all its management members.

19. Can set up a training program (high level) for all members of management on how best to use management documents.

20. And (oh shucks) as a developing generalist, could be a potential president somewhere down the road.

Of course this budding documents officer can't report to someone down low in the hierarchy and still get the job done. The developer can be a man or woman who starts as an assistant to the chief executive officer. In a few cases this person could report to the vice-president of administration . . . if that V.P. is a dynamic, aggressive personality and heads up a strong organization that is respected in all departments.

Your documents developer will write the "big show" document (just the key ones) and then will set corporate document standards for others in departments, divisions, plants or subsidiaries.

This individual will recognize the extreme importance of coordination . . . that no document can be "quality" until it has been through the coordination process with people who will *use* that document. They must be listened to, and each suggestion or objection carefully considered.

The developer needs a sufficient understanding of system design to be able to design a system for accumulating suggested changes — right from the men and women who first see the need for changes . . . from the folks on the "firing line."

The developer will be responsible for the *quality* of all management documents with special emphasis on:

1. Organization charts

2. Statements of work

3. Policies

4. "Big show" procedures (probably from 10 to 20)

5. Authority patterns

The developer will lead all others in the development of their documents by providing standards and supplementary guidance and advice.

Consider, as an example, the role of the developer in organization charting. Developing charting standards requires work. Who will do that work? Who does such work now in your organization? Does he or she report to the chief of the president's staff, to the corporate secretary, to a vice-president of administration, or to the chief executive officer himself? Does somebody in the Personnel Department do this work now? Who develops the company's manuals? Who is the key procedure writer? Is there one outstanding systems analyst in the company? For organization charts the developer must be able to:

1. Develop and provide a standard chart "language" for the entire organization

2. Propose and secure senior management's agreement on names for work to reflect the work packages, including definitions of *divisions, departments, sections, groups,* etc.

3. Develop and maintain the corporate chart and the major departmental charts

If some people (probably scattered) are now doing some of this work, resolve the questions of what they'll be doing in the future . . . and what they will *not* be doing.

The developer will arrange for the physical production of the charts and documents. This work includes typesetting or hand lettering, drafting, paste-up, negative and plate making . . . along with reproduction and punching for insertion in manuals.

The man or woman who undertakes to serve as the developer of management documents certainly needs to understand such intangibles as policy, authority, systems flows, the management process, and the organization's structure.

Further, the developer should know now (or quickly learn) all the basic work functions in *your* organization. The developer serves as a staff worker, does not work in the line, and must be able to converse with any official or with any worker.

RECOMMENDED READING

Out of the thousands of books on the subject of management the following six will serve most fruitfully in expanding the subject of this book *Documents to Manage By.*

1. *The New Playscript Procedure,* Leslie H. Matthies, 1977, Office Publications, Inc., Stamford, CT 06904

2. *Classics in Management,* Harwood F. Merrill, editor, 1960, American Management Associations, New York

3. *Discipline or Disaster,* Magoon and Richards, 1966, Exposition Press, New York

4. *General and Industrial Management,* Henri Fayol, 1949, Pitman Publishing, New York

5. *Management Plus,* Richard Le Tourneau, Zondervan Publishing, Grand Rapids, MI 49506

6. *The Management System,* Leslie H. Matthies, 1976, John Wiley & Sons, New York

Index

191